D1251363

Laurence Duffy and Charles Girard

Like a Bridge
The People of God and the Work of Mary

Rome
1994

Table of Contents

Foreword

Like a Bridge

"You are going to be surprised; I have a great ambition and that is to take hold of the whole world, under the wings of Mary," said Jean-Claude Colin, Marist founder, to the meeting of the policy-making delegates of the Marist Fathers on February 6, 1872. He said that this would happen by means of the members of the Marist family other than its vowed religious. He went on to tell them that "the Blessed Virgin has given it to you to be like a bridge (the expression is not mine) to go to souls, to sinners. Never have people shown such eagerness to go to the Blessed Virgin, and at the end of time there will be but one kingdom, the kingdom of the Blessed Virgin!" We see how Colin linked Mary so closely with Jesus Christ and the Church that he identified the Kingdom of God as her kingdom, too.

The person from whom Colin borrowed the expression, "like a bridge," was Mrs. Marie Elisabeth Blot, a Marist from Paris. In two letters written in 1868 and 1869, she had spoken of inspirations received in prayer and which she attributed to Jesus: "the Third Order of Mary, the Third Order of my Mother, I had given it to them as a bridge to reach souls." (The Third Order of Mary is a name used at times by members of the Society of Mary's secular branch.)

The metaphor of "bridge" fits the situation in which committed believers hope to bring people to know and accept the Good News of Jesus Christ the Savior — in short, where they exercise their role in evangelizing their world. The metaphor is particularly apt in speaking of the "faithful" who believe that they belong to the work of Mary and that they have a mission to do the work of Mary — the one whom they acknowledge as the Mother of Mercy and Mother of the Church.

Clearly Mrs. Blot was a visionary and Fr. Colin was a prophet. They — and other people who will be cited in this book — inspire us as to who we are called to be and even give us hints as to what we are about, but practical answers to all our questions are not going to pop out in crystal clarity. To be faithful to these inspirations, we have to be creative in the light of the needs of our world and of our Church. Marist Father Edwin Keel puts it this way:

> Colin had an intimation or presentiment of something, of a new Church emerging, that he himself didn't have the language or theology to even think about, or enunciate, much less develop a practical strategy for.
>
> I believe that the real meaning toward which Colin's thinking was tending was enunciated by a young lay woman theologian from Poland. She said something to this effect: Most clergy think and act as if it were the job of the laity to assist the clergy in their mission, whereas *it is really the job of the clergy to assist the laity in their mission, which is the mission of the Church, to witness to the Word in the world, to evangelize the world.*
>
> Colin was beginning to think in this direction when he spoke of the laity as the "bridge to souls," as the ones through whom the Church could reach sinners. In this same direction, Alphonse Cozon (a Marist priest who wrote down the elderly Colin's extensive comments about lay Marists) said it is the job of Marist religious to pass the spirit of Mary on to the laity so that they can bring it to every corner of the Church and world.

Addressing the vowed religious members of the Marist family, Ed Keel proposes two lines of action:

> 1. We need to ask the laity (and I am certain there are a number of lay people, already alive with a spirit of evangelization and sufficiently astute and articulate, among our contacts around the world) *how we can help*

them (with training, moral and organizational support, spiritual sustenance, etc.) to carry out *their mission*.

2. We need to work for a conversion of mind and heart on the part of Marist religious. Our ongoing formation programs must adopt the above turnabout in our way of thinking of our role vis-à-vis the laity. And our initial formation programs must cease training our own people for doing ministry and getting laity to assist them, and begin training them to be servants of the mission of the laity. Vatican II has given Colin the language to say what he "saw in a glass darkly" in his own day: that a distinguishing feature of *Marist* ministry is assisting the laity in *their* mission of evangelization.

Plan of the Book

The book is divided into two parts: *Being Marist* and *Doing the Work of Mary*.

The first part focuses on *Being Marist*, on the character or "heart" that gives life to Mary's work and makes it what it is, in a word, the spirit of Mary, the Marist spirit.

We shall explore what *Being Marist* means through the broad vision of the Marist founders, then through the testimonies of lay Marists (and a few priests) from all over the world. A synthesis is offered in a summary of Jean-Claude Colin's understanding of the Marist spirit and in a reflection on the mission of lay people in today's Church and in the world.

The second part explores some possibilities of what *Doing the work of Mary* may mean. It rests on the premise that Mary's spirit is not an intangible specter but a living reality; it proposes a variety of "models" of how lay Marists embody it — as part of a group or individually — as they do Mary's work in today's world and have done so in the past.

At the end of the book, the sources of material used and the references to citations are given; the purpose of this section is to suggest further reading on particular points. Finally, an index of names and a subject index will enable the reader to return to some particular point.

Beyond the Scope of the Book

This book tries to be suggestive, helpful, and unobtrusive; it does not try to be complete. Some important points are mentioned only briefly; some, not at all. Readers are invited to turn to more basic books for the fundamentals of Christian belief and practice. They are invited to consult other sources for the role of the People of God in the task of evangelization, for contemporary teaching on Mary, for the full stories of the Marist founders, and for other related topics.

This is not the place to furnish the names and addresses of Marist leaders in the various parts of the world, since normal changes soon make such lists obsolete. However, anyone seeking further information can write to:

The International Animator for Marist Laity
Via A. Poerio 63
00152 Roma, Italia.

This is not a manual prescribing what is to be done; whatever may be said herein about structure or strategy is offered as a stimulus to the creative genius of people in their various cultures. As Ed Keel said above, it is up to the People of God to articulate their own sense of mission even as there is mutual sharing of Mary's spirit with Marist religious. It is up to all Marists, both religious and those "living in the world," to work out the possibilities inherent in their collaboration in the Church's mission. Groups of lay people in each locality, region, and nation design the shape which the Work of Mary takes among them.

For Whom This Book Is Written

This book is addressed to everyone interested in the Marist spirit and in the way people live it, thus to the general public and particularly to those Marists living in "secular society," as well as to Marist religious, those Sisters, Brothers, and Fathers who share with them the spirit of Mary.

It is for those people who know little about the Marists and their spirit but want to learn more of what it is about.

It is for lay people and diocesan clergy who have heard of the Marists and like their spirit and want to learn how they can begin to have a share in it.

It is for those who have already become part of the Marist movement and want to know more about its past, what it was like in the early days, and about its present and its future.

It is for every family who has a daughter or a son attending a school in which Marists are involved. It is for everyone associated with Marists in a mission or a parish. It is for anyone touched by them in any way.

It is for those of the People of God who, as they spread the Good News of Jesus Christ and share in the evangelization of our world, want to do so with the Marist spirit, in Mary's simple, unobtrusive way.

It will hopefully be informative for the casual reader. Many parts are suitable for personal reflection, for group discussion, or as a springboard for deeper study of the role of lay people — Marists in particular — in their Church and in their world.

Part 1
Being Marist

Chapter 1
An All-Encompassing Vision

Origin of the Idea

About a dozen young men — most of them in their last year at the Saint-Irénée Major Seminary in Lyons, France — had come into the room of one of their teachers, Father Jean Cholleton. It was during the school year between All Saints' Day of 1815 and July of 1816. The group had gradually formed around Jean-Claude Courveille, an older seminarian who had come the previous year from the seminary of Le Puy. Courveille claimed that Mary had spoken to him in his heart and had let him know that, as she had been present at the birth of the Church, so she wanted to be present at this critical time in the life of the Church. Among those who accepted Courveille's story as an invitation from Mary, the first was Étienne Déclas. Étienne Terraillon also responded with enthusiasm. Marcellin Champagnat saw here an opening for the teaching Brothers he had been dreaming about. Jean-Claude Colin told himself, "Now this suits you." Keenly aware of the erosion of religious practice due to the previous century's philosophical currents and the upheavals of the revolution in whose aftermath they had grown up, these young men were eager to reconcile people with God. Terraillon recalled that in these early meetings they talked about the privilege of being

Mary's first children and about people's great need. And Colin, when he later referred to the original inspiration from Mary, would add these words as hers, "My embrace will be open to all who wish to come to me."

When the time came in July 1816 for most of them to go from the seminary into active ministry, they pledged themselves to work toward the foundation of the Congregation of Marists in which they would give their all "to save souls." They saw the key to this aim in Mary's universal "embrace," for this would be Mary's work. The "work of Mary" was not only what they did; it was who they were. They became aware of the spirit of Mary as the life-giving and identifying principle of their project. Colin, all his life long, would keep referring to Mary and her spirit as the model and criterion for the way Marists should or should not act, for what they should or should not do.

Like the Branches of a Tree

The new "Society of Mary" would do the same things that the Society of Jesus (which had been suppressed until that time) had done, but in a different way. Mary's spirit, her Society's spirit, would be simpler and more humble. Also unlike the Jesuits, whose society consisted of men only, the Marists would be all-embracing; they would be like the Carmelites, Franciscans, and Dominicans, with three "orders" for male religious (priests and helper-brothers), female religious (sisters), and people "living in the world." Colin probably contributed to this idea because of his familiarity with a book by H. M. Boudon, who outlined a broad spiritual association certainly not limited to priests and religious. Thus, those who planned the Marist project saw it at first as something like a tree with three branches, but Champagnat asked that there also be another branch for teaching brothers, and so, before too long, Marists began to develop in their four branches. Several years later, a fifth branch, the Missionary Sisters, would begin when women of the Third Order of Mary went to the missions in Oceania.

The original idea was to have a single "Society of Mary" with various branches, including one primarily for lay people; and such was the plan presented to the Holy See in 1833-1834. The Roman authorities, however, considered the framework impractical. Approval came to be granted for separate religious congregations: for a Society of Mary composed only of priests and helper-brothers, for the Marist Brothers of the Schools, and for the Marist Sisters. The branch composed mainly of lay people was, in fact, the first to receive the blessing of the Holy See with a grant of indulgences in August 1834. The Fathers' branch was next, receiving papal approval in April 1836.

The Secular Branch

The Marist project was meant to reach everywhere, for it aimed "to take hold of the whole world, under the wings of Mary"; it meant "to make the whole world Marist." This was possible only because the all-encompassing vision of the Marist project went beyond religious congregations of women and men to include people who "live in secular society." Colin, speaking in 1837 of the Blessed Virgin as "the mother of mercy," said that she was "open to all kinds of people." The all-inclusive Society of Mary, with its secular branch, would ideally be co-extensive with the People of God united under the auspices of Mary.

This means, in most instances, those of God's People other than vowed religious. By what they do and say, they share in the universal mission of revealing to the world that its Savior has come to bring hope and salvation.

Diocesan Clergy Included in the Secular Branch

The People of God, of course, also include ordained ministers who serve and lead in the assembly of the faithful, and these are the secular or diocesan clergy, who are also invited to embrace the Marist spirit. In the early rule drawn up by Colin in 1833, special pious practices are recommended to the priest members of the secular confraternity. Many diocesan priests, like St. John

Marie Vianney, have become members. Among the testimonies presented below, in chapter 2, are some from diocesan priests who have taken on the Marist spirit.

Name

Alphonse Cozon, a young Marist priest to whom Colin was pouring out his ideas on the Marist confraternity of people living in secular society, was amazed at the autonomy Colin wanted each local group to have and asked if there would be any unity. Colin answered: "There will be uniformity in the spirit, but not in the practices. ... Unity will be in the name and the spirit." By this he meant simply the name of Mary and the spirit of Mary. Actually, the secular branch of the Marist family goes by a variety of names. This branch is equal to the other branches, and we all share the one charism, mission, and spirituality.

In the earliest discussion of the project at the seminary in Lyons, France, as we have seen, inspiration was drawn from the medieval model of three "orders" for male religious, and female religious, and people living in secular society (the third order); and so the name "Third Order of Mary" came to be used for this branch, at least through August 1833; but, when Colin made a summary of the Society of Mary's rules for formal presentation to the Holy See in December 1833, he called it "the confraternity of lay people living in the world" instead. In a letter written that same month, he refers to "the associates in the Third Order" and to "this confraternity." In August 1834, the blessings of indulgences were given by Pope Gregory XVI to the "Confraternity of the Faithful or Association under the Auspices of the Blessed Virgin Mary for the Conversion of Sinners and the Perseverance of the Faithful," and this same full name would be used by Colin in 1874 in the "constitutions" he drew up for this branch. Though Colin was not satisfied with the name Third Order of Mary, this name came to be the one commonly used, even by Colin himself, and its usage was somewhat reinforced by the confirmation given it with this name by Cardinal de Bonald of Lyons in 1850.

In 1874, Colin said, "it is not a third order; we are not an order, so we cannot have a third order. It is a confraternity, a society." The name of Third Order is not quite suitable not only because the Marist congregations are not "orders" (they make simple vows, not solemn vows), but also because the Marist confraternity aims to be more than the traditional third orders. Like the latter, it is a part of a spiritual family in whose spirit it shares, but it goes beyond third orders with its broader scope, for it is the principal means for extending the Marist way throughout the world, for making "the whole world Marist."

While the name Third Order of Mary and the aims and organization traditionally associated with it remain valid and acceptable for one aspect of the Marist secular branch, it does not express for the whole body the broad compass of the founding inspirations. In the latter half of the twentieth century, other names, such as Marist Fraternities, Marian Apostolate, and Marist Way, have come to be used as well.

Is there a single name universally applicable to the secular branch of the Marist family? The names **Lay Marists** and **Marist Laity** have become widely used, but their acceptability is conditioned upon a certain understanding of the words.

In correct, canonical terminology, the "laity" are distinguished from the ordained clergy; thus, professed religious Sisters and Brothers are in fact lay people. Still, in popular terminology, the term is used to distinguish most of the People of God not only from the clergy (diocesan or religious) but also from those lay people who are religious "professionals," Sisters and Brothers who profess vows as religious.

In some minds, "laity" has the negative connotations of what people are not. As Marist Father Jan Snijders notes, "We do not know how to define 'lay' except in negative ways: non-cleric, not in holy orders (which puts professed brothers and sisters among the laity), non-religious (which leaves the religious nowhere!) ... If the laity has come of age in the Church then theology will have to do better than define them as 'is not.'"

Unfortunately, no one has found an alternative name for the People of God who are neither clerics nor vowed religious.

The teaching of the Church's second Vatican Council gives dignity to the status of the lay person. The dogmatic constitution on the Church stresses the Church as a communion in which "each individual part of the Church contributes through its special gifts to the good of the other parts and of the whole Church." In that same document as well as in the pastoral constitution on the Church in the modern world, the Council also affirms coequal discipleship, a universal call to holiness, and the autonomy of earthly realities. Leonard Doohan summarizes the Council's teaching as one which "avoids any split between clergy and laity, acknowledges that laity share in the responsibility for the entire Church while not holding office in the organization, and affirms that the earthly ordering of temporal society is the specific way in which a lay person seeks the kingdom of God." (Chapter 4, below, will offer more ample reflections on the laity in the Church.) With this understanding of the word — and only with this understanding — the terms "lay" and "laity" are valid for designating over 98% of the People of God. It is in this sense that these terms are used in this book as part of a commonly accepted name.

The other part of the name is Marist, a word derived from the name "Mary" with the suffix "-ist" (meaning "adhering to" or "advocating"), and so it simply designates "persons who belong to Mary and promote her way."

Whenever there is no ambiguity or need to indicate a distinction of roles, the simple name **Marists** can and should be used; otherwise, the names **Lay Marists** and **Marist Laity** are universally applicable, while each local and national grouping does well to use a name more suitable to its particular aims and culture.

Chapter 2
Lay Marists Speak

Lay Marists from all around the world have said what it means to them to be a Marist. From the following selection of testimonies, you can get a feel for how the spirit of Mary works within the lives of the individuals who reveal themselves in these pages — young, old, single, married, widowed. Along with the statements of lay persons are a few from diocesan priests associated with them. You may be able to identify with some of these varied experiences and insights.

Dr. Anthony Imbrosciano lives in New South Wales, Australia, and teaches philosophy at the Catholic Theological Union in Sydney.

I came to know and appreciate the Marist way of life through my contact with the Marist Fathers at Villa Maria seminary in Sydney, where I lecture in philosophy. What was immediately apparent was a certain subtle, yet clear way of doing things — a particular charism. What deeply impressed me about the Fathers was a certain calm in the way they went about their business — a sense of solidity blended with patience and serenity. It was from my direct acquaintance with them that I became motivated to read the works of their founder. This reading explained the spirituality which fuelled their basic attitude behind the way they did things. Colin himself immediately struck me as a man of great vision for the Church, prophetic, with a profound understanding of the relevance of Mary to our modern theological outlook. What also became apparent was that the basic principles which underpin this Marian attitude can be adapted and lived out in everyday life. Indeed, central to Colin's understanding was a notion that the Marist way of life could be appropriated and lived out by anyone who feels that it provides the fullest possible expression of their relationship with God. I thus came to view the Society of Mary not as something which one joins, but something which one lives out — a particular manner of relating in our world. To this day, I am constantly encouraged and challenged to live out this charism in my everyday life.

Ana María Figueras is from the Marist Parish of Santa Eulalia de Mérida, in Entrevías, Madrid, Spain.

My name is Ana María Figueras. I am 24 years old and come from Madrid, where I was baptized in a parish in the care of the Marist Fathers. At the age of 13, I got involved in a music group in the parish, and a Marist Father invited me to join a group preparing for confirmation. So I undertook a journey that would last five years, during which my life was changed very much.

I discovered the importance of the life of Jesus for my life and that I have a part to play in the Church. I began to take up my responsibilities, to deepen my faith, and to put myself before God to do his will. I thank Jesus and Mary for making me so aware of the plan of God and for doing this in the parish community. I wished to be a committed lay person in my community or wherever I might be.

It was only some time after that I became a lay Marist. I knew that the priests of the parish were Marists, but I had never been too interested in learning about the meaning of this "family name." Three years ago, some youth from the different Marist works in Spain met together to coordinate joint activities for young people and children. Then I began to understand what it means to be a Marist.

What attracted my attention most was the form of Mary's living — her unconditional *Yes*. I asked myself if I could become somewhat like her. I participated in another encounter of lay Marists and I felt that God was asking me to become a lay Marist. At this stage I felt myself launched!

It was not easy for me to try to be like Mary in thought and action. Working at something produces results, but trying to do so anonymously is not easy at times, but I stay with it. I am involved as a catechist for confirmation with the intention of evangelizing young people.

I still have much to learn about the charism and the spirituality of the Society of Mary. I feel happy that I have been able to see that my vocation is to be a lay Marist, that I have placed God at the center of my life, and I have been able to come to Jesus and to his brothers and sisters by way of Mary. I want to be active in the Church without anyone noticing my presence. I want to be like Mary and follow Jesus like her.

Mrs. M. Uemura is 77 years old and lives in Takada, Japan.

When I hear Mary's words "I am the handmaid of the Lord," I feel like the handmaid of a handmaid, a very small person who needs a lot of courage to accept God's will. I ask God each day for this grace and I believe he always provides the help needed. During the past year my husband and his sister who lived with us both died within two weeks of each other. I now live by myself and now realize how lonely life can be at times. I just can't imagine how I would cope if I did not have the gift of faith. I have been a Christian for 55 years and I feel so grateful to God now for having made me part of his family. Now more than anything else I want to be able to live my remaining years in a useful way, sharing with other people what I have received through so many precious life experiences. I want to live for people, quietly and lovingly, as Mary did.

Bronwyn and John Reynolds are a married couple with two teenage children. Bronwyn ran a Marian Mothers group (see pp. 135-137) for 7 years. Both of them are in the core leadership team of a new Marist Family group in Sydney, Australia.

We are attracted to the Marist laity because we consider Mary to be an important role model both in the Church and the family. We consider that quietly spreading Mary's influence is a very important mission of the Marist family. We also consider *it* important to follow Mary's example of following Christ's words and work. We think we are able to do this by participating in setting up family groups within our parish. Although the group is in its very early formative stage, we believe there is a need in the Church for like-minded families to join together for both spiritual and moral support. We also think that having Mary as a model is important because she had the gift of true understanding of faith to which we all aspire.

Ms. Paula Pearce was born in 1951, lives in Kent, England.

I have only been a regular member of the Hythe Marist Way for about 18 months, but this time has been a turning point in my religious development and life. As a child I had early experiences of spiritual richness, and Mary, our Mother, was for a time of great comfort every day. However, during teenage years I lost any sense of devotion to Our Lady and went through a serious adolescent crisis, part of which was a spiritual crisis.

From student days my interest in practical Catholicism was, on the surface, quite strong. I was an active member of the Catholic Society and the St. Vincent de Paul Society, a student on courses run for the laity (including a Diploma in Theology), a member of the Catholic Marriage Advisory Council. As my adopted children went to school, I returned to teaching and became responsible for Traveler Education — throwing me into new causes and gaining the confidence of the communities. At times I became smug because I was very dependent on my own resources.

In my work I managed to establish communication between an Irish Travelling community and the local Church. Clergy visited the site and the children attended the local Catholic primary school (not without teething problems). This coincided with my need for a regular prayer group. I was told about the

Marist Way. I also joined a pilgrimage to the Marian Shrine of Knock.

From that time I became freshly interested in Our Lady and became dissatisfied with the tensions I was experiencing at work. An illness gave me time to take stock and I decided to return to straight teaching, without responsibility other than as a teacher. My experience of living through some vivid experiences of Traveler culture and hostility towards the travelling community for 3 years made history teaching seem very distant. I had taught religion as a minor subject and I was a catechist. So when a post was advertised for a religious education teacher in a Catholic Comprehensive school, I applied.

It does not seem to me a coincidence that my change in career direction followed the deepening of my interest in Mary. I went on another Marian pilgrimage and joined a Marian Peace Day in Aylesford during summer 1992 — since then the focus of my life has changed dramatically. I had attended Marist Way meetings regularly since my first attendance and became increasingly part of the local community. (I found out that my family had been enrolled in the Marists when I was a teenager!). The meetings focused on the rosary, scripture reading and informative "lectures" from Sr. Kevin. I found these helped my prayer life. However I needed to become more committed to prayer and so sought a spiritual director who helped me to begin to pray with the Bible. I also went to some courses and joined a weekly prayer group. I loosely follow the Medjugorje suggestions of prayer, penance, rosary, fasting (partial — not just bread and water), and I attend daily Mass.

So it's hard to limit my testimony to the Marist Way. This group certainly gave me a new outlook and my other experiences connected with Mary have combined to give me a living personal faith, which I feel began two years ago, but was only confirmed when I changed career and experienced the Shrines of Walsingham, Knock and Aylesford last summer. I have had a feast of Marian-inspired experiences which have led me *ad Jesum per*

Mariam [*to Jesus through Mary*] — or rather have put me on the first stages of the journey.

It is only now that my joy in the faith, my trust in the Lord and my genuine efforts to center my daily life on prayer, have begun to bring an inner peace. "Late have I loved Thee" has been my motto since last summer but Mary was the springboard and the Marist Way my regular base for early stages in my spiritual development. I praise and thank God that I have a strong devotion to Our Lady — shared by my sister and being shared with others.

I have a tremendous affection for Sr. Kevin (and Fr. Curran) in our parish. She has put considerable effort into directing our group and I personally find the new directions she leads us in are very relevant to my own growth. I see Mary's work for me being present in a range of experiences which have made an impact. I have been able to develop at a gentle pace and I feel I have been enfolded in her arms and held on the wings of the Lord since my commitment was sealed.

Gabi Dölzer lives in Germany.

Being a Marist has given direction to my life for over ten years. I got to know the community of the Marist Fathers when I went to the prayer group that met in their house. I was still young and seeking for meaning and faith in my life. In the prayer group I got to know two priests whose manner of dealing with people baffled me, was new to me at that time. Today I would call it "an advance of trust" in people, or maybe that I experienced in these men something of God's love for his people.

At that time I used to frequent other spiritual communities as well, and got to know the "free churches" also. Nowhere else did I find so much acceptance, so much freedom in myself, as I did in the community of the Marists. To me it was a key experience to be able to see my uniqueness as a human being and accept it. This happened to me through the Marists.

Because of this deep experience, no wonder that I wished to belong more closely to this community, to live this spirit and this attitude.

Today, twelve years after, I am on my own way as a lay Marist, having come this far in spite of detours and wrong tracks. For me to be a Marist has always meant to "open doors and gates" in order to be able to breathe, in the Church and in the presence of God, where there is room to find my own place as a lay Christian. I hope to follow the way I have started, right up to my death, knowing well that our God is the friend of humanity.

Pierre Saumet (who writes below) and his wife Chantal belong to the* Fraternités Maristes, *Paris, France.

In the context of practicing Catholics, our home is not exceptional. During our adolescence we were involved in Christian organizations: my wife with the *Jeunesse Étudiante Chrétienne* (Young Christian Students), and I was in the *Scouts de France*. After our marriage, five children took up most of our free time. I was also exercising a profession more fully (fiscal adviser), and doing further studies in accounting.

Nevertheless, one of us was involved with the *St. Vincent de Paul* and at the *Centre des Jeunes Patrons*, and the other in a group of *Action Catholique des Milieux Indépendants*.

Our moving to Lyons for professional reasons led us to meet again a childhood friend, who drew us to participate in a meeting of families which had a Marist Father as spiritual director. Having heard of a possible grouping of lay Marists, and having studied the spiritualities of other groups of evangelical life, we decided to join the *Fraternités Maristes*, which at that moment were in a time of change:

- the constitution of one movement at the national level (Paris and Lyons).
- the creation of an association, the responsibility for which belonged to the lay people.

- the adoption of a spiritual rule characterized by great flexibility.
- the development of a review entitled *Lettre aux Fraternités Maristes* [*Letter to the Marist Fraternities*].

We were involved in this evolution. Coming to Paris for professional reasons, we were immediately integrated into a group in the making.

What appeared to us as very positive in this belonging to the *Fraternités Maristes* was the possibility of Christian reflection as a couple, helped by other members, on the different problems of life and the evolution of the present-day world, the problems of society (unemployment, poverty, attention to lonely, elderly, and sick people), or the problems of professional, civic, ecclesial life — such as life presents daily.

What we drew from the Marist spirit was the preponderant place given to welcome, good-will, openness to others, to all others: children, parents, friends first, but also colleagues at work, neighbors, foreigners come to France to work, etc.

It is in this attitude that we found the strength to bring a response of action, or, at least, a movement of sympathy. It is in this way that we have been led to get involved with catechetical groups, groups of parents and students, associations of welcome for visitors, union groups.

Andrea Pichlmeier has studied theology in Germany and Ireland. She has made a particular study of Marist spirituality. After working with the Marist Fathers in various kinds of retreats in Germany, she has begun studies for a doctorate in theology.

How did I become interested in the Marist way of life, and what does it mean to me? To be quite honest: had I been searching for a spiritual group or way of life I probably would not have "found" the Marists. As a liberal-minded student of theology, any Marian spirituality — viewed from outside — might have caused fear of a traditionalist narrowness in me. But it was not by mere information that I found the Marists. It was through personal encounter and relationships that the Marists found me. A few scholastics, studying the same years as I, invited me to their house. It was persons and personalities that attracted me and made me interested in the way they live. But, no, this would be too short an explanation. Friendships came before a spiritual identity or even the search for it. My personal Marist history teaches me that it is by way of human experience in relation to others and to the immediate personal world that God writes the spiritual history of a person, giving direction and meaning even to mere "accidents." But was it mere accident that the Marists I met during my studies in Passau (Germany) and Dublin (Ireland) embodied such a gentleness, openness and welcome, empathy and authenticity — most of them to a high degree as individuals, but also as communities? It has been an experience of Church — more important for me than I realized at the time. Who knows — would I, as a woman theologian, have turned my back on a male-dominated Church somewhere along the way? The Marist sense of a Christian and pastoral identity became a real alternative for me: a "female" approach, humble, yet without losing the dignity of the person.

Over the years I had the opportunity to become more familiar with Marist spirituality by translating texts and also trying to express my own thoughts on the Marist sources — a work which I hope to continue and which helps me to understand my practical pastoral work and supports it.

So far I have described my "Marist motivation" mainly from the point of view of a theologian. But this is only part of my Marist reality: the large network of relationships, responsibilities, of personal support and the sense of belonging to a family which I would not like to miss anymore. It is the large dimension of experiencing God present between us, in the relationship — feeling, thinking, judging and acting like Mary.

Charles Jenkinson lives in Hull, England.

To be a Marist means to me a constant talking with the Mother of God. Frequent reference to her attitude to her Son as a mother, gives an easy attitude to Jesus and allows me to be embraced by him in great love. He becomes a near and familiar relative in a close family union. The fruits of love, understanding, patience, etc., are the fruits of the spirit made real in me.

Frequent reference to her attitude to her Son as a disciple curbs inclinations that are obstacles to holiness. Mary's total acceptance of the will of God as Father, Son or Holy Spirit is the model for my spirituality.

But being a Marist means more. There is always present the knowledge that being Marist is the result of a positive response to her call. I am aware of it. I do not know yet what the implications are, but it is an abiding expectancy of the things to be revealed and the things to be achieved on her behalf. Meanwhile, her love and love from the Society of Mary nurture this sense of mission and the importance of sharing with others her way to Jesus.

P.S. I can only point out that the Marist Way Rule and meetings with daily meditation underpin everything I've said. It seems that we know enough about Marist spirituality — the big question is how to inform people in concrete terms of how it can be achieved.

Guillermo Múñoz Lara, a chemical engineer employed by a manufacturer of electrical cables, lives in Mexico City, Mexico; he tells of his life as a layman in the Society of Mary.

Like most adolescents, around the age of 14 to 17, I felt very self-sufficient and I forgot about God, and I even recall sometimes denying God and attacking the Church with childish jokes. "But something happened to me, a meeting by chance did change me... You came into my life; and my soul took refuge in you." I write these lines, remembering the lyrics of a song we sang at a

Festival of Christian Song. Yes, indeed, God keeps for each of us that moment when we meet him again, when he shows us that the parable of the Prodigal Son can still recur these days.

I was invited to a "Marist Retreat" at Campo María in the city of Cuernavaca, state of Morelos, September 25-27, 1981, and I attended. On this retreat, I opened my heart to God, and, during the Mass on Sunday the 27th, I strongly felt his presence at the time for the exchange of peace and so I fell to my knees and cried with emotion. God the Father had run up to me and embraced me. I was 17 years old and my conversion had taken place. It meant a great deal to me that this significant moment of my life had occurred during a Marist retreat. What did the Virgin Mary have to do with all of this? What message did she have? I discovered that the Virgin Mary had something very great in store for me.

After the retreat, I went to the C.P.P. (Centro Politécnico de Proyección), which is a Catholic youth center directed by Father Pedro Herrasti, S.M. After only a few days, I was invited to a Christian Life retreat from October 9 to 12, 1981, and I went. It was a most beautiful experience of God, and it was then that I finally came upon God's message for all humanity: "God chose us ... to be holy and blameless in his sight, to be full of love" (Eph 1:4). There was a point in the retreat when the Virgin Mary was presented; at that moment, those present were invited to make an offering to the Virgin. That was a meaningful moment for me because of what I had experienced in the Marist retreat, and I offered my entire life to the Virgin and asked of her that I might be a Marist all my life. Perhaps at that time I was not aware of what it meant to "be a Marist all my life."

Among the whole community at the C.P.P., it was soon evident that we wanted to adopt the Marist spirituality, particularly because the priests there are Marists. This harmonized quite well with my offering. Father Herrasti, our spiritual director, suggested founding what we call the Marist Family, but we were faced with questions like "how, who, when?" The C.P.P. community held a meeting so that those of us who were interested might begin to bring this idea to life. We began to meet on Sundays and we gradually gave shape to the idea, as we decided on meeting days, schedules, promises, duties and rights in what we call the *statutes of membership* and, naturally, our spirituality was based on numbers 49 and 50 of the Constitutions of the Society of Mary.

It was good that Father J. C. Colin included lay people in his plan and allowed for the possibility of forming what other spiritualities call a third order. It is not that it is formed of third-rate Christians but rather of first-class Christians who are committed to God and his Mother, the Virgin Mary.

There are about twenty Apostolic Groups in the C.P.P., each of which has its own objectives. Our work within the community was to share Marist spirituality with all of them, to strive so that every day they might love the Virgin Mary more and finally one day might decide to become part of the Marist Family. For this, the Marist Family was entrusted with having an annual retreat for all members of the C.P.P., and we obviously had a Marist retreat, in which we entrusted the retreatants to the Virgin Mary as Mother, model, and intercessor of them all. It was a very beautiful experience and our Marist Family grew with the help of these retreats. We structured this retreat by following the *Ideario Mariano* [*Marian Ideas*], written by Father Antoine Forissier and Brother Basilio Rueda for the Archdiocese of Mexico City in the Marian Year of 1988, proclaimed by Pope John Paul II.

All of us members of the Marist Family were very happy to be entrusted with coordinating for the C.P.P. the retreats held during Holy Week, and with giving them a Marist focus by bringing out the role of the Virgin Mary in the Pascal mystery. The retreats were very successful, and many in our community took an interest in becoming Marists, for they discovered a Mother who loved us so much that she entrusted us to her own Son, in the same way as God our Father has done.

In all honesty, it was rather easy to insert the Marist spirituality into the community. All were quite pleased to accept that spirituality which we follow very closely since the Fathers of our community are Marists. Another big help is the fact that we Mexicans hold deep in our hearts that we are *Guadalupanos*, favored by Our Lady of Guadalupe, since for over 450 years our Empress of the Americas has left us with her image impressed on the cloak of Blessed Juan Diego.

Our belonging to the Marist Family has helped us to take up many pious practices, such as praying the Rosary daily, the Angelus, frequent confession and communion, reading of the Word of God and of the Virgin Mary's life, and living "unknown and indeed even hidden in this world." I don't remember exactly when it happened, but we learned to sing the *Salve Regina* and the *Regina Cæli* in Latin and they are really beautiful.

God granted me the grace of marrying a woman who was engaged in the same apostolate as I (Christian Life retreats), but, even more important, she is also a lay Marist, and so we are on the same frequency. Leticia and I have a very happy and holy marriage in which we put God at the head but the Virgin Mary is like our right arm.

One of our most beautiful experiences as a married couple was to be invited to belong to the *Equipos de Nuestra Señora* (*Our Lady's Teams*), a movement founded in France during the present century to promote the spirituality of married couples. Naturally, when we were to give a name to our Team, all of us members chose the name of *Holy Name of Mary*. It is obvious that the Virgin Mary holds us in her protection and embrace. She is always at our side, helping us to meet all our needs. What a great blessing it is to have such a mother! I remember how, during the birth of our son Guillermo, all those who were there (doctors, nurses, the anesthetist, and helpers), asking God and the Virgin Mary to be present, and, while the baby was being born, we were praying and singing. It was a magnificent experience of faith, especially at those moments when one senses that one is an extension of the Creator in being able to give life to a new being. Thanks be to God and the Virgin, it went well for all of us.

In our daily life, the Virgin Mary is always present. Our spiritual director is a Marist Father; our apostolate is with the Virgin Mary in Our Lady's Teams; in every church in this country there is always the image of the Virgin of Guadalupe in addition to that of some other title; in our home we have a small altar dedicated to the Virgin Mary, and even at work I always have a picture of the Virgin Mary in sight.

"Am I not here maybe as your Mother? Aren't you perhaps in my embrace and protection? What more do you need?" (words of the Virgin Mary of Guadalupe to the Indian, Blessed Juan Diego on the hill of Tepeyac).

Oh Mary, all we have to do is to continue holding on to the good fortune of being called to belong to your Marist Family. Thank you, Father Colin, for having thought of us lay people and for having founded the Society of Mary.

The Marist way of a lay Marist — February 1993 — Yolande Cantù lives in London, England.

Since its inauguration in June 1868, the Church of Notre Dame de France in London has been under the care of the Marist Fathers, who came from France on a mission of service to French immigrants. One of the waves of immigration towards this city brought my mother who, in 1928, married my father, an Italian, at Notre Dame de France. Having been baptized at Notre Dame de France, catechized by the Marist Fathers, and made my first Holy Communion in this church, I could say that from the cradle I was a Marist. Without really knowing it, of course.

To know so, I needed 40 years. Each one of us follows his/her own particular spiritual path. I followed mine for a long time at a distance from the Marist ambiance. A type of nostalgia which I could not explain well led me back to Notre Dame de France on the death of my mother, and it was only there that I saw and understood the value — and the difference — of the Marist way.

First I appreciated the friendship, the listening and the simplicity of the team of Marist Fathers at Notre Dame de

France in the 1980's. To them and their dedication I have a debt of gratitude. Perhaps it is also in human nature to wish to promote what and whom one admires. But in this case, admiration was the last thing which the priests wanted to attract ... hidden and unknown. Little by little I learned.

To be a Marist, especially as a lay person, especially as a woman, means working in the shadow of silence, for practical example often speaks louder than words. It means being humbly available as Mary was — her *fiat* is the highest example. It means being a vehicle, a catalyst, a sower without desiring to be the harvester — to God alone be the glory of the harvest.

But this does not mean being passive. Being hidden and unknown, one has a genuine and sympathetic regard for the poor, the isolated, the ill, the stranger — who are often, perforce, hidden and unknown. We know that the option of God is for the poor. "Happy those who know they themselves are poor, for the Reign of God is theirs."

The gospels speak little of Mary, who is indeed hidden and unknown. Nevertheless, the right to sing the *Magnificat*, the culmination of the victory of all those whom God loves, is hers — she sings it in the name of the poor and the humble.

That is the ideal. The reality of daily life is more sober. I work, under the auspices of the St. Vincent de Paul Society, with old people. As much as possible, I have always looked for a "helping" employment, and I consider myself fortunate to have always found something suitable. I help a little in the parish, in little things. Nothing special. As many others do.

Bill Rae manages a transport company. David McKeown works with the handicapped. Both live in Wellington, New Zealand.

For us this is what it means to be Marists:

▪ to be recipients of a special grace to participate in Mary's work in the world and the Church.

▪ to be blessed by the care and protection of Mary in the world and to be guided by God — and by looking at Mary as our model and example — in the decisions of our lives such as: career or vocational choices, relationships, place to live, temporal, financial affairs.

▪ being a member of a wider, international community / Marist family responding to the call to evangelisation, and evangelising in a quiet, low-key way in our homes, workplaces and amongst friends.

We find ourselves dependent on the grace of God to live this and we find prayer of particular importance to respond to Mary's words: "Do whatever he tells you."

Young people from Sénégal, in Africa; they are part of a lay Marist group.

The example of Mary represents for us a manner of living the gospel in a humble and self-effacing way, but without weakness. This is important in the context in which we live in Sénégal. Mary teaches us to live our faith in a strong fashion among our Muslim brothers and sisters who are a majority — avoiding ostentation. She invites us to an attitude of reserve in the face of all that is too prominent, showy: one does more things by not showing them too much.

To live the Marist spirit, is to let God work in us, to give him *carte blanche* to direct our actions and our thoughts as he did for Mary. It means saying, like the Blessed Virgin: "Yes, Lord. I do not understand, but I keep going."

Her example encourages me: the smallest choices are of value, even if they don't appear too great. The inanity of things often strikes me as well as the vanity of showiness, of eye-catching ways. The model of Mary who serves without expecting any return satisfies me, invites me to follow her. She is like a second chance for youth.

Mark Walsh is in his 30's and lives in Australia.

Marist laity, to me, means belonging to the Body of Christ in a particular way, with that group of Catholics who choose our Holy Mother Mary as their model and guide in seeking Christ. It is a call to belong to the family of Marists as a lay member of that family. It is a call to take on the identity and ideals of a Marist and become enmeshed in Mary's ways, particularly and especially in the way I live out my lay vocation within my family and in the church community.

Marist spirituality is that particular way of coming to know and love Christ through the person of Mary, not that Mary is an end in herself but a means to an end in Christ. It is to have a faith which believes that Mary knows and loves Christ perfectly and only desires that we follow in her way. Her way, which she offers as a model and guide for us all, embraces a central devotion to prayer, humble service to others, and a simple lifestyle which includes penance and fasting.

My call to have a Marist lay involvement came about through contact with a Marist priest and an invitation to be involved in part of his ministry. This has brought about, on my part, a choice to strive towards Mary's way. This has led to my involvement in the "Marist Family Ministry Team" which, for me, includes working in the areas of personal, family, and parish ministry. In personal ministry, I seek to have prayer, the sacraments, scripture, and an accountability in conscience a central part of my life. In family ministry, I seek growth in relationship with my immediate family members and in the wider parish and church community. I have been involved in presenting renewal weekends for other Catholics.

Mr. Yasunohu Oka is a 48 year old schoolteacher who lives at Nishiyamato, Japan.

In life there are more painful and bitter and hard things than delights and pleasures. This is true of me. There are more cases when I am not sure that God is with me. Especially when I am in great distress, he seems to be out of my sight. He seems to be silent about the questions, "Why do you treat me in such a way? Why don't you grant my requests? Why do you desert me?" Frankly speaking I wish I could keep away from carrying his cross. It is often too much for me.

Once I disliked and rejected the cross with his body because it was so cruel and horrifying. I gave just a symbolic meaning of his sacrifice and death to it. But now, as I grow older and become more involved in various pains and hardships, I have come to think of it as a symbol of His deep love for me and the people. When I am down and weary, I feel quite relieved and tranquil to see the cross. It tells me, "I am your Saviour. I am with you. I am sharing your suffering."

Mary, standing by the cross, endured his crucifixion and accepted it. I think it was due to her strong and absolute confidence in God. I wish to follow her example. So I pray to her that whatever hardship and difficulty I may face, I will be able to accept and endure it. I am sure our attitude with such humbleness and reliance upon God's love will move his will. And none of our sorrows and pains will be lost, they will be revived in his love.

Mary is so full of mercy. When I pray in earnest, she sends me some persons who can give aid and support me, without fail. She is taking the role of his intermediary. Apart from the question of need, she also gets us a lot of chances to encounter splendid and good people who help us grow up and develop in faith and in mind.

Anne Maughan lives in Ashford, Kent, England.

I joined the Marist Way 33 years ago while I was still at school and was an isolated member until a group was formed in Hythe. Being involved in a group has helped me a great deal spiritually. Reading passages from the Bible, reflecting on them and discussing them has increased my understanding of the Bible. Before the Old Testament and the Psalms had very little meaning for me. I now use my Bible as a way of prayer, especially the Psalms.

The same way with the rosary. The rosary used to be a repetition of the Our Father, Hail Mary and the Glory be. Now with reflection on each mystery, each decade has some bearing on the way in which I live my life. It has become more meaningful, encouraging me to try to live my life like Mary — impossible I know — but maybe I can just pass on a bit of Marist spirit to those around me.

Benoît Gaussens from France speaks of his experience, particularly of a meeting held in August 1993 of young adults in Jarsy.

I would like to begin by thanking my parents for having introduced me to Notre-Dame of Bury, a Marist secondary school in France. Reluctant to enter it at the beginning, I had five marvelous years there. Five rich years of apprenticeship in *life*, through moments of joy, and also of despair. Five years of discovery of the Marists.

This year the meeting of young lay Marists at Jarsy was an occasion for reflection on this Marist spirit and for exchange of experiences on our way of living it.

I have a wonderful memory of this week as one of peace and sincerity. I learned much about life and I realized the hidden importance of the Marist education which I have received.

Today, I know that this Marist spirit is for me a constant strength on which I can count every moment, high or low, of this I am sure.

After the example of Mary, I understand that this spirit does not search for glory, but tries to understand events, tries to be present at important moments with the greatest discretion, tries to follow and support those who are in need, and finally tries to live in the Church positively and fully, and not in lamentation and sin.

I came back from this "retreat" transformed, in the depths of myself. The meeting at Jarsy was the first attempt at a gathering of young Marists. The result was very encouraging.

Extracts from letters of Conveners of Marian Mothers Groups in New Zealand. The organization of these groups is described below (pp. 135-137).

▪ There's no denying the tremendous blessings we've seen in the lives of the mothers and their families. The Lord seems to be restoring us and giving us new strength in our roles as mothers, wives, child bearers. Friends and I can see this group as being most helpful in getting our husbands together, too.

▪ I know of no other women's organization which fills a void for us Catholic mothers who really want something "meaty" for our discussion and to provide us with spiritual support.

▪ Our group has always enjoyed the tapes and gradually more confidence has been established between us. Now there is lively discussion. I am very grateful for the support and spiritual growth fostered in me by our group.

▪ The average attendance is around ten mothers. The meetings with the tapes are fruitful and ten minutes listening isn't too long. We've been pleased to take up the offer from older women, to entertain the pre-schoolers who wish to be entertained. The women who came to us from the coffee morning group say they really get something out of Marian Mothers.

▪ Our group is helping the mothers to be more positive in our approach to motherhood and to understand the gift we've been given. I have been attending Marian Mothers for a year now and have learned so much. The most amazing part for me is about Mary. We have been taught nothing about her these days and we're lucky if she gets a mention even at Christmas! I see now what I've been missing all these years. Thank you also for the tape about her which has brought her back into my life. I am a solo mother and Mary is becoming very special to me.

▪ I find the material very interesting. I didn't know many of the women for a start. It's a joy to see a lot of the women opening up with their problems and it makes me realize I am not alone with mine. I have also made a lot of close new friends.

▪ The last meeting when we played the tape on Mary was well-received and enjoyed. It gave most of us a new and refreshing image of Mary which we liked and certainly found easier to relate to. That tape is doing the rounds of the parish and the RCIA (Catechumens) group and is at present in the hands of a Presbyterian mother. We have several women who come regularly and are not Catholics but are committed women in their own Churches. We've just finished a wonderful week praying for unity amongst Christians, culminating last week in a joint worship service in the Presbyterian church.

Marcelo Lavares tells us below about himself. He lives in the Philippines.

I'm Marcelo Segundo Noyo Lavares, 31 years old, single. I was born in Manila, but our family now lives in the south of the Philippines. After graduating from High School in 1979, I underwent two years training as a catechist. This was followed by one year working in family apostolate, and then worked in a parish called Kalamanisig mainly with tribal minority people in the mountains giving them basic reading, writing, arithmetic and religion. I learned many things from them also, especially their simple way of living.

In 1984 the Marist Fathers took over the administration of the parish and I continued my work with the tribal people but also branched out more broadly with catechesis in the parish. This continued for four years. Then I proceeded to College to study for a bachelor's degree in arts. During the summers I kept up my contact with the Marist Fathers, working with them in their mission. By this time I had come to know the Marists well — their community life, spiritual life, and charism which they lived together as a family.

They mentioned to me about lay Marists, and I was curious to know more. When Fr. Philip Callaghan explained it to me, I was very interested; and, being an adventurous person, I wanted to follow it up. When a chance came to help the Marist Fathers in their vocation work, I took it up as a lay Marist. I am studying the Marist spirituality and charism. I have really learned many things, and now I am a lay Marist no longer because of adventure or curiosity but because of life. As I mingle more with the Marist fathers and undergo this formation, my principles and values are changing.

Leny Hasimoto who gave this testimony is from São Paulo, Brazil. Her friend, Berenice Bueno de Sena, who is involved in the same Chanel Group, gave a similar one.

My first contact with the Marist family was in 1972 when I was studying at a college of the Marist Brothers. Later I participated in the activities of youth groups at the college. We had meetings and gatherings, and helped in the preparation of those who were to receive the sacrament of confirmation. A time came when our meetings changed and we began basing them on biblical themes and other topics of interest, in addition to planning pastoral action.

After an inactive period, we decided with Fr. Bertrand Huot (a Marist priest) to begin meeting again with the addition of new members. Fr. Bertrand gave us some information about the Third Order of Mary and invited us to join it. The group, made up of couples and former coordinators of youth groups at the Marist college, accepted this new idea. So the Chanel Group came to be, honoring St. Peter Chanel.

The example of faith, dedication to neighbor, humility, simplicity, and the desire to serve inspired the Chanel Group to meet regularly so as to deepen religious understanding and to grasp the role of lay Marists in the Christian community. In time, we felt the need to move towards something practical. At that moment also we invited others to participate in our group. Through Fr. Bertrand we came to know of a remedial teacher who did excellent work with mentally deficient children. The group was enthused with this new project and decided to collaborate in the opening of a new school for these children. Little by little as we meet, we are in the process of organizing ourselves and soon hope to open this school.

Françoise Reynès, a lay Marist from Toulon, France. Extracts from her testimony.

When I came to know the Marists I was relatively old (already in my 50's). I was enthusiastic about my profession as a civil Judge for children. Ever since I left off being involved with Scouting, I was looking for a group that could enrich me spiritually. After many attempts in different groups, I had the good fortune to be invited to an evening at *La Cordeille* (the school of the Marist Fathers in Toulon). Although I was wary, for I had bad memories of certain Catholic schools, I had the impression, from the first gathering, of finally having found a Church according to my heart, a Church which put Vatican II into practice, and which did not present the most crying faults of the Church of my childhood, the Church which I had rejected for almost 20 years — throwing out the baby with the bath-water.

Lay people, Sisters, and Marist Fathers met together every week for a friendly gathering which comprised a meal, a discussion on a given subject, and a prayer celebration. Everyone, priest, sister or lay person, had his/her role. Cooking, dishes, serving the meal, animating the discussion — everyone shared. The priests presided at the celebration, but without any pomp; rather, they considered themselves just like anyone else in the group. We were far from being a docile flock, being "sermoned" by a cleric issuing forth unquestionable truths.

In the course of the years, the first impression has been reinforced, and now I like this Society of Mary, in which the Church presents an honest face, a joyful face, a merciful face, a Church where clergy and laity mutually evangelize one another, trying to form themselves better to go to the poor, and to pray alone and together in simple yet beautiful celebrations.

I love this living Church, on the move, which gives a prominent place to simplicity, openness, and service. It is there that I have learned to see Mary, in all her simplicity, in the light of the gospel, unencumbered by the folderol of an inaccessible Queen, and whom I can approach and take for a model.

I am no longer crushed, tending towards an impossible perfection, but sustained, loved, helped in a way leading to a God of love. Thanks be to the Lord, to Jean-Claude Colin, and to those who have taken his heritage into their lives.

Susan Corless, Wallsend, England, participates in the Marist Way.

We have gained a better understanding of our Faith, especially the converts, by our prayers, readings and discussions. Our discussions are now more open and so we are all learning.

Corinne and Bernard Fenet, husband and wife, live in Toulon, France. Both are involved in a Marist Fathers school. Bernard has been ordained deacon. Corinne tells about their Marist journey.

Our Marist history goes back to 1978 when the director of a secondary school (the Lycée Champagnat) was looking for a teacher of philosophy. My husband was looking for a teaching position. A providential friend made the connection. Nearby was La Neylière, a house of the Marist Fathers.

What did we find at La Neylière?

▪ A warm welcome for us with our faith, doubts, and desire for involvement. I remember the baptism of our children in the heart of this community — priests, sisters, laity — living!

▪ Openness to the questions which trouble the world, our Western society, as well as local problems, including those of our immediate neighbors, the farmers. I remember well the weekends of reflection on topics such as "the couple," "non-violence," "the Third World," "quotas for dairy farmers," etc.

▪ The value of community life (through the association, Friends of la Neylière), inviting everyone to give the best of themselves and reveal their talents.

▪ The value of prayer where everyone had a chance to speak and there was respectful listening.

It was among the Marists that we have discovered across the years our place in the Church — a place at once of drawing to the sources and of being sent on mission. Speaking simply we asked them to be sent on mission, and they simply accepted our request.

After La Neylière there was La Cordeille (a Catholic school near Toulon). There, too, we found a place of community life, priests and laity together, which is indispensable for us. It is there that we became officially Lay Marist Associates. For Bernard, as he met marginalized and little-loved youth there, it was a time when he discovered his vocation to become a deacon, and he has since been ordained as deacon.

For today what matters is the transmission of the love of God which was present in Mary and is the Marist treasure. What kind of a Church will do this?

- A Church welcoming all: Christians and non-Christians.
- A Church attentive to the needs of the world and not only to those of heaven. At Cana Mary did not say "They have no more holy water," but "They have no more wine."
- A Church which is discreet: "She did not cause anyone to talk about her, and yet how much good did she not do?" (Mary, by her actions and doubtless, too, by prayer).
- A Church concerned with the poorest people, as it is to them first that Christ asks us to be attentive.

The Congregation of Marist Fathers can pass; we can pass; but for the moment that is given now together, it is our concern that this Church will not pass, because it is that of Christ.

Joachim Laufenberg is from Cologne in Germany.

I got to know the Marists through Bernd Kordes and his confreres in Cologne; Bernd was a "normal" fellow student, and the house in the Hochstadenstrasse, a normal parish residence. And yet, there was something different about it or maybe more visible than elsewhere. I got the impression that I belonged to them and was accepted by them without any fuss. I found that I was welcome, felt somehow at home. That is what I always seem to feel whenever I am in a Marist community. The way we treat each other, religious and lay people, is a delight to me. Our spirituality, with Mary being our Mother calling us and wanting to accompany us on our way to a life with and in God, really struck me as a Christian.

There was an external reason for me to become a member of the Third Order of Mary. A girl student, Eva R., entered it: what I did then was a consequence of my own innermost being. My decision grew and developed within me rather than being a particular call or coming from a special insight. I did feel a call; it was like a gentle "lure" or a "gentle seduction" (Mary?), rather than a call that would shake me and confuse me or even capture me.

I have never regretted my way as a Marist or even questioned it, because I feel that it is the right way for me and my future. Every day I enjoy this fact.

Mrs. Breda McGee lives in Dublin, Ireland.

In terms of the Church in Ireland I have done some unusual things. In 1986 I did a pastoral course at All Hallows, Dublin, and have worked in retreats and as a facilitator in pastoral reflection groups. It was in 1986 at the pastoral course that I met the Marist seminarians Gerry Kane and Luke Monahan. I am not the pious type, so pious or unearthly religious, Marist or not, would have made little sense to me. But something about these men impressed me. I was trying to express new depths of spiritual awareness and awakenings. I could not find a name or title for this. But one experience I had during my All Hallows year was what I call my bridge experience. I found I could listen to and understand the pain and joy of the religious I was mixing with; while at the same time I could equally understand the voice of the alienated. Many of the friends and family wanted nothing to do with God or Church. The experience lasted for months in a variety of forms and it represents an important time of growth for me. My present knowledge of Mary's action in my life comes from that time. I got to know more Marist Fathers and became involved as a lay adviser to their formation program. I was able to attend the Marist Colloquium in Rome in Easter week 1992.

I have changed profoundly in the past year. When I write that down, it "sounds" as if some disruptive action happened. That is not the case. The change I refer to is quiet and easy and it is taking no effort of mine. I have an assurance of peace at present which gently landed on me and at a time when so much around me is in turmoil — big changes in my family and a number of deaths and difficulties on my street. (A seventeen year old boy hanged himself virtually in my garden just after Christmas. I was the one the neighbors came to, and I ask myself why? Well — just because I was there!) Deep inside me I find a new stillness, and when I feel closest to God I am always aware of Mary. It is as if she were my humanness. She represents my drive towards God, my way of coming into relationship with God. She represents for me a way of living that does not push others around, does not force others to change, but brings a deep contemplative attitude to bear on situations and helps me to be a bridge in life.

Heinz Gerd Bieber joined a Marist lay group (called Marian Apostolate) on November 14, 1991, in Germany.

November 14, 1991, is the day that I regard as the most beautiful one I ever experienced. Considering how everything began:

At the age of 7, I was sent to a home for orphans, with four of my sisters and brothers. The upbringing there was Catholic — and there were lots of orders and bans! When I left that home, I learned the profession of a nurse's aid. I believed it to be God's will, and I had within me a great longing for Jesus Christ.

However, problems developed. I witnessed the enormous suffering in the hospitals. I was ill myself with asthma. Psychological problems developed and then alcoholism. Finally I had no flat, no job, no more relationship with human beings. My relationship with God, not to speak of Mary, was dead — for many long years. But deep within me I felt that there was somebody carrying me. One day I had reached the bottom level of my life — when someone came along asking if he could help me. I said yes and suddenly I was prepared to change my life. I was able to say yes to life, to prayer, to my fellow human beings, to God, to love.

At that stage I went in for therapy and went to Church every so often. I got a flat and worked as a male nurse in an old people's home. It was then I got to know the "heart of Jesus" in the Church. Help came through a woman who introduced me to a Bible-sharing circle and to Marist life. The people there got more and more familiar to me and more lovable. I got to know Bernd, a Marist Father, and to appreciate him a lot. Here in this circle, I got to know Mary the Mother of Jesus and her attitude. I did not want to become a "Marian fanatic," but I learned what it means to be a Marist in the lay group — a Christian trying to live the Marian attitudes and make them his own, e.g., being merciful towards myself, towards fellow human beings, towards old and sick people; turning to God who is all, and Jesus Christ who is my Master.

I could feel: together with my sisters and brothers I can be the one I am in truth, a human being who tries to think like Mary, to judge like Mary, to feel and act like Mary. Somehow I get the impression that I am on the right way — from my contentment. God is the one who gives. I am the one to accept what he gives me, and to be prolific in being there for other people, taking Mary, our mother, as a model.

Helen Hulten lives in the United States of America.

Helen Hulten, wife of a former Senator of Hawaii, a member of the Third Order of Mary for many years, said that she always had devotion to Mary which she learned from her mother. As a teenager she was asked by a Dominican priest to join the Third Order of St. Dominic, but at that age she was not interested.

Later in life she was asked by Joseph McGettigan, a Third Order of Mary member at Star of the Sea Church in Honolulu, Hawaii, to join and she accepted the invitation. She has given conferences on Our Blessed Mother to the Sodality in her parish. Her husband has also joined the Third Order of Mary.

Pepita Sánchez is married and she and her husband consider themselves to be lay Marists. They live in Coslada, Spain.

I would like to say something about how I discovered the Marist spirit, and then to say something about how I live it.

In the first place I would say I had a strong attraction for the form of living and preaching of Christ which a small group of Christian priests had. (They were Marist Fathers but I did not know that yet). This prompted me and my husband to undertake a way to mature our faith and to begin to work with them and other lay people for the Reign of God.

On this journey, I kept receiving the message of Christ very strongly and directly, and yet the Marist spirit was also filtering into me, without my realizing it.

Later on, in a meeting of lay Marists, we came together from different places with one thing in common: we were in contact with some Marist community and we were attracted by their style. There we were able to give a name to what they had transmitted to us in the attitudes of daily life: the spirit of the Society of Mary.

I discovered that Mary was more than the image I had of her as rather passive and perhaps too "sweet"; it was an image which brought to my life as a Christian almost nothing from which I might gain strength to be an exemplary believer and follower of Christ.

Being a Marist does not mean having special devotions to Mary; it means working as she did and in her style. Deep within me, the conviction began to grow that my decision to follow Christ should now be joined with that of doing so in Mary's way because the whole world and each one of us need to live by the values proposed to us by the Society of Mary as the means for reaching God as we build a new world.

Mary animates me constantly to follow Christ, to trust him more, as she trusted, to be humbler and to listen to myself and those around me with my heart, to express the tenderness that God has put in me, which sometimes I hide, and to be active in serving motivated solely by love, and to be a witness of the mercy of God, above all, among people who are most marginalized, without being noticed, like Mary.

Some reflections from Nicola Perrone Pacifico about Fr. Colin's ideas. Nicola is a layman who lives in Italy.

What was most characteristic of Colin's life was his spirituality, the intuition he drew from the *ignoti et quasi occulti in hoc mundo* (unknown and indeed even hidden in this world), and the message he left to his Society: one of interiority, of poverty, precariousness and apostolic communion.

The other important aspect of Colin's adventure is the topicality and relevance of his basic insight. What he discovered in the wake of the French Revolution is precisely what groups of Catholics are looking for today as we approach the year 2000: to live in a hidden way in fraternal communion: the silent but active presence of Mary.

Today various groups of laity are aware of the need for evangelization, for a deepening faith, to help humanity to know itself. They wish to become pastoral workers, evangelizers to the new poor and the new marginalized. A hundred fifty years ago Fr. Colin had already seen something of it. He was a precursor of that impulse to evangelize which is at the root of today's apostolate movements. The Society of Mary can now fulfill its mission by simply vivifying its original spiritual heritage, by remembering and living out in practice: love and understanding, the warmth of Colin, imitating the spirit of Mary in the service of the newborn Church.

Nilda Stela Merino Campos is from Callao, Peru.

My name is Nilda Stela Merino Campos. I am a 23-year-old Peruvian and at present I am finishing my teacher training with the intention of using it one day as a lay Marist missionary in the abandoned areas of Peru and elsewhere. I have belonged to the Marist Missionary Community (*see pp. 120-122*) since it began, and at the present time I serve as animator of the Community. (The religious act as advisers).

Since I came to know Mary, at home with my family and at college, I wanted to love her and know her as a protecting mother. Since my adolescence I belonged to parish groups. I was also in a missionary group. On one occasion I was invited to a meeting where Marist spirituality and the missions were talked about and where we prayed together.

Through my contact with the Marists, I discovered a Mary I had not even imagined. By belonging to the Marist Missionary Community, my experience of God became richer in the light of Mary. For me, to be a part of the Marist family means to be truly Church and to form community, like Mary among the Apostles: silent disciple of Christ, sharing her love among them. It means I feel I am Church in the lay state.

I feel called to live in a simple manner, moving unobtrusively into action, hidden and unknown, attentive to the needs of others. It means being missionary; allowing myself to be guided by the will of the Lord in order to live my faith and to share the gospel with those who hunger for bread and hunger for God, to let myself be evangelized by the poor, to come to the most marginalized and neglected.

In a few words, it means discovering a human Mary and living her life, as she is present in the Church and in the world — a Mary who teaches me to live loving Christ, with all that means. She animates and accompanies me in daily life, in study, in prayer, in friendship, in recreation, in the running of food centers for the poor, of centers for women's welfare, of evangelization and mission for our rural communities in the Andes.

The following anonymous testimony comes from Hawaii in the United States of America.

Over ten years ago I first learned of the Society of Mary and the Third Order from a dear friend who was a charter member of the Confraternity when it was first formed in Honolulu. Because of a physical handicap, making it impossible for her to drive, I took her regularly to the monthly meeting at Star of the Sea Church, including all days of recollection and other special celebrations. She regularly spoke of Marist spirituality and the way of Mary, telling me of the love and spiritual healing it had brought her. She wanted me to experience the same joy and constantly asked me to consider becoming a member of the Third Order. I explained to her many times that I was not a "joiner." I did not wish to join the group just to say I belonged.

In the summer of 1983, I spoke to Father Flynn of my interest in the Third Order. He welcomed me and after some discussion referred me to the Mistress of Novices for an interview and a year long period of instruction. With a number of others similarly imbued with a deep and sincere love for the Mother of our Lord, we met monthly for a year of instruction and prayer. In August 1984 we were professed and became members of the Third Order of Mary.

At the time I did not know and truly understand what Marist spirituality would some day mean to me. I had, however, begun a journey down a dimly lit passage stumbling often, trying to follow Mary's way. I gradually realized that it was not enough to be drawn to Mary as the Spouse of the Holy Spirit, but I needed to understand her as the "model in Faith."

I believe what appealed to me then and has been more fully characterized since, is the apostolic style of the Society of Mary. It seems to me that the humility, compassion and service, all Marian attributes, are reflected over and over in the day to day activities of the Society of Mary. As a lay member of the Society I have tried to follow Mary's example in devotion, acceptance and obedience to the will of God.

I continue to read and reflect on the gospel message that I may understand and follow the vision of Father Colin. In doing so I trust that I will continue to realize more fully the spirituality of the Society of Mary and the Third Order. Each day I try in prayer, reflection or meditation to look back at the significance of being united with Mary in faith. Perhaps to dream of the future in faith, yet always to remember that unless Jesus and his Blessed Mother are walking by my side, my dreams are unlikely to come to fruition. Perhaps many of the dreams are unattainable — that does not matter. What is important is that I can dream. I am able to visualize goals which reflect new insights about the importance of placing my trust in God, of listening always to his voice, knowing that if it is his will, I can reach those goals. I pray that the Blessed Virgin Mary will continue to walk with me, leading me always in the footsteps of her Son, that I may be better fitted to do his work and hers.

Peter and Joan Griffiths are lay Marists living in Toowoomba, Australia; their three sons are teenagers.

Marist lay people see themselves as having a mission to support the whole Church by supporting those within their range of contact to become wholesome and loving members of the Body of Christ, as Mary lived her mission of supporting and nourishing Jesus and his Church during their time on earth. Marist lay people have a caring and concerned mentality with a strong sense of outreach to others and tend to work with simplicity, "quietly" and "in the background" to get things done. Being Marist gives us a feeling of homecoming and welcome, a belonging to the broader Church family, a melding between religious life and family life; a connectedness and a team spirit mentality is developing, with an ownership of the necessity of laity's involvement in the well-being of our church.

To us the Marist spirit means allowing Mary to take us to her Son, living our lives in such a way that we become attractive to others and draw others to Jesus through Mary's way, a simple prayerfulness in the living out of our lives, with a discipline both in personal and public life. It means adopting or developing a sense of mobility: when one job is done, pass the reins over and move onto the next. It also means mobility in the physical sense, a willingness to travel to others, a willingness to walk the extra mile, a willingness to be mobile in mind, attitude, and physically to serve others in the spirit of Mary. It means acknowledging Mary as our mother, allowing Mary's involvement in our daily life and decision-making, an openness to listen to Mary through others and recognising her there. It means embracing Mary's hospitality and compassion for all. It means a sense of joy and wonder for the beauty of God within us and others, and around us.

Everything we do is flavoured by a Marist spirit and vision. Our involvement means being available to accompany people on their faith journey, i.e., through Marriage Encounter, Marist Family Ministry Team, youth support, faith education through the parish, religious education in schools, etc.

Within our family unit, we have found the following to be important in maintaining a caring, loving, and Lord-centered environment: Open communications, particularly around the family meal table; couple prayer and family prayer. Couple prayer needs to be in addition to family prayer. Morning family prayer has been very significant in establishing a peaceful tone of the whole of the day for the family. In our case this is only a couple of minutes together after breakfast before the family disperses on its different tasks for the day. We have experienced more success in family prayer with short focused times rather than longer periods, part of getting used to the idea in changing our lifestyle! Also important is focusing on each other's gifts and making use of these in family decisions and activities — fun-making, making memories, affirmation, clarity of ideas, respect for each other. There is family discussion and decision making on the use of resources and time, i.e., family activities, use of TV, celebration, holidays, recreation time, major purchases. All family members have input on these, without our relegating our responsibility as parents.

In the broader community, among the things we try to do is the development of in-home programs to share with other families on issues of family concern. The in-home programs are designed for families to take away so as to use the same methodology in developing their own sessions focused on their specific family issues. These programs involve all family members. We have found that, where the children are actively involved, the families start to work together and own their own family spirituality. The family units see that there are other families that are working in this way and this reduces the effect of peer pressure from the world, particularly amongst teenagers.

We have good response from our sons with their involvement in these types of things. They have seen and experienced the joys and benefits of this type of relationship. They have particularly noticed and commented on the effects of lack of family prayer on our family's interpersonal relationships!

Pauli Fischer lives in Cologne, Germany.

As a young girl in East Germany I joined a Marian association of young women, and like other Catholics was devoted to Mary. Through the Marists in my parish here in Cologne I learned another way of imitating Mary. Lay Marists took me to seminars at the house in Ahmsen; and I always came back fully enthused by the simplicity and the family atmosphere there. Apart from Mary's simple way I was impressed by her belonging to the disciples after Christ's death, her taking part in spreading the good news, and her task not only to live *with* but also to live *for* others. I had always wanted to live in such a community. That is why I became a lay Marist.

Clive Dean from Middlesbrough, England.

My involvement with the Marist Way has helped me deepen my existing devotion to Our Lady, and through greater understanding of the place of Our Lady in the Church, to understand more clearly the difference between Catholic and non-Catholic spirituality.

Involved as I have been in ecumenical activities, the absence of Our Lady in God's redemptive plan from the minds of our separated brethren has struck me very forcibly. Without the consent of Our Lady and her continuing involvement in that plan, something very basic to the Christian faith and God's plan of salvation is widely overlooked.

Clearly, the devotion to our Divine Lord among our fellow Christians would be strengthened and better understood if the part of Our Lady, as the vessel of the Incarnation, was more widely disseminated and the honor due to her as Mother of God more widely spread through ecumenical literature and personal contact.

Antón Niñe Fernández is from Spain.

When I was still a child I came to know the Marist Fathers and their activities; and I saw their work through displays, photographs and publications — as something good and attractive. Time passed and all the dreams and illusions of my youth went forward, step by step, with Marist activities: marches, gatherings, celebrations, camps.

This way of doing things, with simplicity, with transparency, attracted me. I have to say that on some occasions I did not see this simplicity, but I believe that everyone — including Christians — has highs and lows in his actions — and Marists do, too. I saw that this failure in simplicity was overcome by their self-abandonment and dedication.

The Marist spirit increased in my life: at work, in sports, and in other activities. When I reached maturity and analyzed the meaning of things — especially their value — I asked myself: Will I be able to participate in this work with greater depth? I wanted an answer from within myself. It was not easy, but I made my decision: yes. It was a personal commitment to collaborate with the Church and the Marist family.

As I made this decision, other questions arose: How can I transmit the Marist spirit to others? The response was clear: yes, Antón, if you involve yourself (participating in the life of the Church and life in society: catechesis, sports, cultural activities etc.).

I confess that this involvement has its foundation in the serenity and purity of the heart of Mary, always present in my life, and that is where I look in analyzing all I do. Of one thing I am sure: that I am a companion on the way with other men and women who work in the Church, in the community, with commitment.

Mrs. T. Miyano is 56 years old and lives in Nishiyamato, Japan.

I was thinking recently about the fact of Mary being patroness of Japan and what a strange coincidence it was that both the beginning and the end of World War II took place on Marian feast days. Sometimes I wonder how much extra sadness and suffering that must have caused her. The Marist Fathers have taught me to pray simply and directly to Mary and to ask her about such things. During my life there were times when I distanced myself from God and from Our Lady, but amazingly God never fails to reach out and draw me back to him. And this frequently takes place through people whom I meet. Twenty years ago I came with my two small children to live in Nara Prefecture, the region my mother originally came from. That was my first meeting with these priests who live with Mary's spirit in their hearts. I soon noticed how the Marists were so humble, unassuming and warmhearted. I began to learn how to relate with Mary and as it were speak with her in prayer. "What are the things I too could do? What would be the best thing to do now?" I feel deep gratitude to the Marists who share this spirit with us, and I pray daily for them.

Fr. Renato Frappi, S.M., tells the story of how the witness of one group led to the formation of a new group in Italy in 1992.

The community of Marconia has seen the birth of a new group of lay Marists. The idea was born a little while back, when a small group of Marist tertiaries of Rome were in Marconia on the occasion of the perpetual profession of Emanuele Di Mare (a Marist seminarian at that time). By contact with them, some people of Marconia came to know of the possibility of lay Marists and told Fr. Franco Messori, the parish priest, that they, too, wanted to belong to this Third Order of Mary. He was happy with the proposition, and in time it happened.

After a suitable preparation, 28 persons became committed to the idea; and, on September 8, 1992, a feast day of Mary, during a solemn celebration, they professed publicly to live according to the spirit of the Third Order of Mary.

Domenico (Mimì) and Paola Della Speranza, a married couple from Marconia in Italy, tell what becoming Marists has meant to them.

When the pastor offered those who so desired the opportunity to belong to the Marist Third Order, the satisfaction of many of us was truly great. On September 8, 1992, after a triduum of preparation, a sizable group of women and some couples became part of the greater Marist family.

For us in particular it was a moment of great emotion. We had always had a strong devotion to Mary: our marriage was celebrated in May, Mary's month; the first name of our two daughters is Mary. Now to belong to the Marist Third Order was for us truly a cause of pride and joy.

Prayer meetings attended by both the Third Order members and our Marist priests are held on the most important feasts of Mary, on the anniversary of the death of the father founder of the Marists and on the anniversaries of the most important moments in the history of the Congregation. It is wonderful to be together on these occasions, to pray and to experience the sense of belonging to the greater Marist family.

"To think as Mary, to judge as Mary, to feel and act as Mary" will be for us, Third Order members, the goal toward which we will aim with the help of our heavenly Mother and her beloved Son.

Jennifer Ritchie, a practicing Anglican, became a Marist through contact with the Marist Sisters in Australia.

My name is Jen Ritchie, and I am a practicing Anglican, worshipping at St. Faith's Church, Burwood, Melbourne. Although I lived in the same street and suburb as the Marist Sisters for 23 years, I had never met them. One day, by chance, I met a Marist Sister at the Christian Meditation Network (John Main) group. Then Mary the Mother of Jesus gradually became a real part of my life. Now I am bringing her into the lives of my husband and three grownup children and all my friends of many different religious persuasions. Mary is the one I go to in all my difficulties. I love saying the *Hail Mary*; and, when I was in Tasmania visiting my son, I met a little group of Catholics who taught me how to say the Rosary.

I see myself as a little pilgrim of Mary, going through the world in a very ordinary, simple way, trying to help those especially loved by God, the poorest and most wounded people. Mary, too, was a housewife and at Nazareth lived so closely with Jesus and Joseph. I help my husband, who has a small textile business, and I became a fully affiliated Marist in the chapel of the Marist Sisters, with my dear friend, Sister Romanus, present. She helped me in so many difficult moments; now she is in heaven! Through the Sisters, I met and became a friend and retreatant of Brother Andrew of Calcutta (co-founder with Mother Teresa of the Little Brothers of Charity); and now I go as often as I can to the Little Sisters of Charity's Fitzroy refuge for abandoned and abused women and children, and also am a part of the healing ministry team at St. Paul's Anglican Cathedral in the city. I say to my friends, "Why do we bring Mary into our lives only at Christmas? She should be there always bringing us to meet Jesus in all the events of our lives and in all the people we meet." I thank God that I am at home with the Marist Family in Melbourne and can share in their special days and the celebration of their yearly feast, Fourviere.

Joe Nainima, a Marist layman from Ba, in Fiji: his story is related by Sister Loyola, S.M.

In our Marist lay group in Ba, there is a man named Joe Nainima. He has a great love for Our Lady, and whenever we meet, Mary is the topic of our conversation. Joe goes to socialize with the parish men in the evenings but waits his opportunity to talk to them about Mary. One evening he sat and drank *yaqona* with some Methodist men and spoke to them, too, about Mary our Mother. They were so impressed, they went home and told their wives. One day soon after that, some Methodist women came to Joe and said, "Come and talk to us about 'the Mother' because we don't have the Mother in our Church." Joe came to Father and to me to get "the blessing," then, with a few women from our group, went to the village hall where he spoke to the Methodist women about Mary; and the hall was packed.

Kevin Luxford, a Marist layman, is the Animator of the Marist Laity in Melbourne, Victoria, Australia.

The Marist Laity embodies a lot of the very far-sighted thinking of Jean Claude Colin. Colin is really a person for today. Marist Laity is not exclusive; it is warmly inclusive.

Marist Laity is not fanatical, or harshly ascetic. It does not impose strange ritual, rigid practices, long prayers or devotions. It is balanced, sensible, practical, and totally orthodox.

We need many models of Church even to begin to have some appreciation of what Church is. As Church members, we need to accept that leadership and authority, especially with respect to divine teaching, is necessary. But as baptised and confirmed lay members, we also have to be aware of and to live other models of Church, especially Church as *servant*, helping the poor, the youth, the disadvantaged, the sick and the dying, and Church as *herald*, proclaiming in word and deed the good news that we have been reconciled with our Creator and liberated from the effects of sin and death. We lay people need to recognise our calling to be missionary. Marist Laity provides the ideals, training, spiritual formation, mutual assistance and encouragement to live our missionary vocation.

Marist Laity is attractive; it works because it addresses basic human needs and wants. It offers a "what-you-see-is-what-you-get" living, working model of its ideals.

Marist Laity is a way of helping Church make an impact on our immediate environment by our basic Christian/human love. (I was very taken by Nell's unsung visits to women often abused; this is a unique ministry, something which I doubt many priests or other males could do effectively.) [*Nell is a Melbourne Lay Marist in Kevin Luxford's group.*]

Marist Laity does not blow its own trumpet and seeks to do good quietly and unobtrusively. This has two important results: (1) the members are not asked to do anything extraordinary, so what we do is well within our capabilities, and, (2) because we are hidden and unknown, we are unlikely to attract unfavourable criticism.

Lay Marist communities of married and single people engaged in prayerful living in common may provide an alternative to the nuclear family and provide succour and hope for the homeless and unemployed.

I like Marist Laity because it provides me with the most effective challenge to live gospel values that I have ever experienced. While externally warm and gentle, for me it is internally confronting. I cannot in comfort continue attending meetings unless good efforts are made to live Christian values in my marriage and in relationship with those around me at home and at work.

An anonymous member of a group of engineers and businessmen and their wives, meeting at the French parish in Mexico City, Mexico.

It all began with our forming a prayer group to deal with our spiritual concerns and our desire to deepen and live our faith better. Several groups already existed in the parish, served by Marist Fathers. It was decided to start a new group with engineers, business men, and their wives. Some of the women were also in business, either working with their husbands or independently. The group soon had twenty members.

Meetings were held every two weeks, on a Thursday evening, in the members' apartments. The sessions began with an hour and a half of Christian reflection, then there was a half hour of prayer around the Eucharist, and finally a social (*convivencia*) in the dining room.

Our meditations-discussions were at first based on the readings from the following Sunday's Mass and later on a book of the Bible, such as the Acts of the Apostles. Other topics were freely chosen at times; its was up to the host couple to choose and suggest texts from spiritual books or even newspapers.

We looked for a common activity for the group, something which would let us work together on these problems. Our search ended in an unexpected way. One night, the cook of one of our couples made her appearance in tears in the living room and explained that she had just been expelled from her small lot of land on which she had built a small house with her savings, which represented twenty years of work. She had purchased the land from communal farmers who had already lost their land, through expropriation by the authorities for a school site. Within a month, the bulldozers were to come and raze everything.

On the whole our group was composed of people of action, who were responsible for employees and engaged in business affairs, but who were also concerned with social problems. After two or three years, the themes discussed came closer to our professional concerns, as we turned to the encyclical *Populorum progressio*, the development of peoples, and the Puebla documents on the Church in Latin America.

She had been given another lot, but she did not know how to go about recovering the material from her old house to build another one on the new land and finance the operation. She had no husband, and her adolescent son was out of work.

We went out to look the situation over and found thirty other families in the same situation. We believed that it was clearly the intention of Providence to send us there. With the help of a social worker from the French parish and with the information we could gather, we began to help some of the families in their acquisition of construction material and, at times, doing some of the work ourselves.

We quickly became acquainted with the local authorities who, with honesty and unselfishness, told us about the most needy families among those originally expelled and then about others throughout the neighborhood. In the helpful climate created, some of us went there on a good many Sundays.

Two and a half years later, with the contribution of funds and work, not only by members of the group, but also by our parish, we were able to contribute to the betterment of some forty families, to participate in half a dozen community-interest projects (paths, a small primary school, retaining walls for the ravine), and to aid financially with the Center of Development, which included a school for apprentices and a dispensary.

Our business lives reaped an important bonus. The experience of a common work had brought us into close contact with the daily life of that section of the city, similar to the sections where most of our employees lived; it enabled us to speak more openly and more confidently of our professional and social problems. Prayer, the Bible, the social encyclicals, and the parish setting laid a spiritual foundation for efforts which corresponded very directly to our vocation as Christian laity.

Fr. Eli Carter is a diocesan priest. He is the director of the Leeward Fraternity of the Marist Laity at Our Lady Queen of Peace, Nanakuli, Hawaii, United States of America.

On August 23, 1975 I was ordained a diocesan priest for the Diocese of Honolulu in the State of Hawaii. I've always thought about being a religious but I've never really talked about it to anyone. My first assignment was to be associate pastor at Our Lady of Perpetual Help Church, in Ewa Beach. It was not an easy assignment for me because things weren't what I thought they would be like. Being a rookie I decided to turn my thoughts and days into praying to Our Lady.

In 1978 a group of women in Ewa Beach had come to me and we began going into scriptures almost daily and we prayed together often. We named our group Our Lady's Prayer Community. I would like to tell you a little about this group because ultimately they all became our faithful Third Order members. By the grace of God each one, as the Holy Spirit willed, had a hunger for prayer, scriptures and community. We craved and thirsted that God's will be done in each one of us. At this particular period we had no knowledge of what the Third Order of Mary was. In fact, we had never heard of this lay branch in the Marist Order.

Mary the Mother of Jesus and our Mother was always invoked in our requests and prayers. She called us together to heal the sick, the brokenhearted, to feed the hungry and the poor; and through the scriptures she promised us that her Son would be with us always. We must love him... we must cherish him... we must do all things in his name. Every week we met to pray. Every week our line grew a little longer. The sick came from all over. Some who came for prayers said that we should belong to this Third Order branch of the Marists. One day an invitation came to have lunch with Ruth Chun. Out of curiosity we accepted her invitation. She spoke to us about the lay Marists. We had to study. We had to pray constantly... and this we did for a whole year. Until today the men and women meet in joy and enthusiasm.

What attracted me to become a member of the Third Order of Mary was the love of God and one another. I was attracted by the sincerity in praying. I was very much attracted by the teachings that were presented. I remember each teaching put us on fire and as a group we were in one mind, one heart and one spirit. I found that the Third Order of Mary is for active, busy people who have a thousand and one commitments and yet feel the need of "something more" in their lives. What attracted me to the Marist life is involvement, not withdrawal. One of our instruction letters tells us that Christ is risen, alive and present in our world, and our calling is to find him in the city. What attracts me in the Marist way are the simple teachings that grow within... Let me reminisce: prayer begins with listening rather than talking, listening is hearing with love, God speaks to us in scripture, God speaks to us in people, God speaks to us in the events of life.

Some words from diocesan priests who have Marian Mothers groups in their parishes, New Zealand.

▪ From a pastoral point of view, the group is invaluable. I get all sorts of information about people in the parish from the mothers — finding out who is expecting a baby, who is sick and many other things. Follow-up visits are made where appropriate. Marriages outside the Church have been rectified. We have women of all degrees of faith present — a solo mother, two married outside the Church, and some with all manner of problems. We have an occasional night when husbands and wives come together socially. I am a great believer in these groups as is the Church herself, especially in Third World countries where I have been able to see them in operation.

▪ In my view the Marian Mothers group is just about the best thing that has happened recently in this parish. The good the women are doing is really impressive.

▪ You'll be interested to learn that this year two mothers in the group were baptized together at the Sunday Eucharist last week. Both were married to Catholic men. I see big possibilities for evangelization in these groups. I hope they spread to many more parishes in New Zealand.

Chapter 3
The Marist Spirit

The "Whole World Marist"

"Well, the whole world would be Marist then?" Cardinal Castracane asked, laughing, and Father Colin answered, "Yes." When the good cardinal understood that the Marist founder really meant it, he was no longer amused; in writing a report on the "confraternity of men and women of every status and from every country," he did not hesitate to point out "how outlandish and irregular would be the plan for this confraternity to spread over the whole world." The cardinal pointed to the implications for international politics, "to the suspicion that might be aroused in princes by a confraternity of this kind." Colin took it all in a more light-hearted vein and often retold the story of this encounter. Twenty years later, as he was addressing a meeting of Marist Fathers' delegates, he recalled the incident and concluded, "frankly, it made me laugh to think that we were going to make governments tremble."

Colin's aim, of course, was not to rattle governments (ruled by princes or presidents), but that "all the faithful may with God's help be 'of one heart and one mind' in the bosom of the ... Church and that all, walking worthily before God and under Mary's guidance, may attain eternal life." Thus he said on another occasion that we must begin a new Church over again, adding immediately, "I do not mean that in a literal sense, that would be blasphemy. But still, in a certain sense, yes, we must begin a new Church." This would happen by gathering everyone together through the Marist lay branch, with whom the Marist religious share the same spirit. We have just heard, in chapter 2, the testimonies of people for whom that spirit has made a difference in their lives.

Spirit

Just what is this spirit? "To live as Mary, feel as Mary, think as Mary" was a prescription often repeated by Colin, according to Alphonse Cozon, who also heard the founder explain: "The name Marist is not an empty title. Come on, if we are Marists, it must be seen in our conduct."

Earlier, in 1842, Colin had written to all Marists: "By our state and duty we are placed in the footsteps of Jesus Christ and of his Mother; let all our thoughts, all the movements of our heart, all our steps be worthy of our august models. Let us live by their life, think as they thought, make our judgments as they themselves did." In other words, a Marist's every thought and action refers back to Mary and her divine Son.

Other phrases characterizing the spirit of Mary, the Marist spirit, were addressed over the years to the lay Marists as well as to Marist religious. Eventually, the basic rule of the Society of Mary, as approved in 1872, brought together, in a section entitled "The Spirit of the Society," a series of brief formulas which evoke this spirit — quotations from the Bible and other short phrases which a lived experience had charged with meaning. The first paragraph (no. 49) gives us a set of spiritual exercises whereby we might open ourselves to the spirit of Mary; the second (no. 50), a set of guidelines whereby we might become transparent in mission. This basic text, given in the Fathers' rule but applicable to all Marists, is as follows:

> 49. Let them always keep in mind that they belong by gracious choice to the family of blessed Mary, Mother of God, from whose name they are called Marists, and whom they have chosen from the beginning as their model and their first and perpetual superior. If therefore they are and wish to be true sons of this dear Mother, let them continually strive to draw upon her spirit and breathe it: a spirit of humility, self-denial, intimate union with God, and the most ardent love of neighbor; and so they must think as Mary, judge as Mary, feel and act as Mary in all things, otherwise they will be unworthy and degenerate sons.

50. Therefore, following in the footsteps of their Mother, let them above all be entirely removed from the spirit of the world, from any greed for earthly goods, and be totally emptied of all self-concern; let them strive to deny themselves completely in all things, seeking not their own interests, but only those of Christ and Mary; considering themselves as exiles and pilgrims on earth, indeed as worthless servants and as the refuse of the world; using the things of this world as if not using them; sedulously avoiding, in their buildings and living quarters, in their life style and in all their dealings with others, anything that might suggest display, ostentation, or a desire for attention; loving to be unknown and subject to all; without deceit or cunning; in a word, acting always with such great poverty, humility and modesty, simplicity of heart, and unconcern for vanity and worldly ambition, and moreover so combining a love of solitude and silence and the practice of hidden virtues with works of zeal, that, even though they must undertake the various ministries helpful to the salvation of souls, they seem to be unknown and indeed even hidden in this world.

Let them all cling fast to this spirit in the knowledge that it is the very pivot and foundation of their whole Society.

The Marist historian, Jean Coste, who has written extensively on the richness of this basic text, concludes his examination with the statement: "We call the Marist spirit that common manner of feeling and reacting which unites and characterizes Marists from the moment they accept to direct their lives in relation to the person of Mary, the intuitions of Fr. Colin, and the living tradition of the Society."

Colin connects the Marist spirit with an original inspiration coming from on high. This gives to the Marist family a basic character to which it has to adapt: it sets certain defining limits, yet at the same time it is the source of whatever the Marist family carries out. Ultimately, this spirit depends on the Holy Spirit of God. It is the Holy Spirit who guided Mary and fashioned her, who inspired and helped Colin to understand the mystery of

Mary, and who, acting within the Church and the Marist family, sees to it that the Marists of today learn how to walk in the footsteps of Mary and of their founders.

Basic Points of Reference

In reflecting on the Marist spirit, we need to keep in mind its basic points of reference, the elementary realities which govern everything that can be said on the subject. In the thinking which guided the elaboration of statements on this spirit, we find two complementary spiritual trends corresponding respectively to the two paragraphs of the text cited above.

The first trend is found to be developed in the first paragraph of the text cited (no. 49). Here, Colin states the fact that the Society (including its lay branch) is the Society of *Mary*. From this attribution of the Society to Mary — an attribution founded on her initial and gratuitous choice, expressed by the very endowment of the name of Marist, and ratified by the acknowledgement of Mary as model and superior — Colin deduces the necessity for the Marist of having the spirit of Mary. Thus, an important point of reference for the Marist spirit is Mary herself, in her whole manner of thinking, judging, feeling, acting, such as she was in the history which can be uncovered in the Scriptures. (More will be said below on the way Marists relate to Mary.)

The second trend is encountered each time that Colin, in speaking about some concrete way of acting, pronounces it in conformity or in opposition to the spirit of the Society. In so doing, he refers to the intuitions which from the very beginning express for him the will of Mary for Marists. The ideas he advances are not his own but what Mary wished for her Society. Thus, a second point of reference for understanding the Marist spirit is the spiritual experience of Colin as founder, that is, the intuitions of the one who felt and defined for us the implications of the Marian spirit along the lines of self-effacement and the lack of pretense and hypocrisy in the our mission.

There is also a third element, Marist tradition. The spirit corresponds to the realization, experienced by Marists as a social body, of the principles which animate its life and action. The spirit is more than a series of formulas; it is the life Marists are ever seeking to live as they inevitably and constantly adapt to new situations.

How Marists Relate to Mary

The relationship of Marists with Mary has been shaped by the inspirations and insights of the founder, Jean-Claude Colin. To what was no more than an abstract seminarians' program, waiting to be filled in, Colin gave a spiritual content and developed an apostolic spirituality of a Marian kind. The Marist spirit is not precisely a new spirituality, for it is not marked by any special prayers or any new devotion. Colin never spoke of Mary for her own sake, but only to put Marists in touch with her. They relate to her in her historical perspective and in her relation to the Church.

"Mary ... support of the Church ... at its birth ... at the end of time," a key founding intuition, is explained by Coste:

> Mary is thus seen in clear relief as in a large fresco that includes the whole history of Christianity; she is seen in relationship to the Church. More hidden than any of the Apostles, she was yet the light and consolation of the primitive Church. In our day, a time of impiety and incredulity, Marists are to do good as she did, remaining unknown and hidden, placing themselves at the service of the Church in the most hidden way possible, without attracting attention to themselves or being preoccupied with their particular position or interests.

Coste goes on to speak of the way in which Mary figures in Colin's thinking:

> She is not there as an object of cult, of honor, of contemplation; nor even properly speaking as an object of imitation in the rather organized and external form that this expression so often suggests. ... In basic passages of our

> constitutions, Mary ... appears ... in expressions that imply participation, identification: "... they are ... indeed even to live her life." "Let them continually strive to draw upon her spirit and breathe it ... and so they must think as Mary, judge as Mary, feel and act as Mary in all things" (1872 S.M. Const., nos. 1, 49).

Our relationship with Mary consistently leads us to seek the good suggested by Mary's life rather than to devote explicit attention to her. With Father Colin the Blessed Virgin is meant to be seen essentially in her relation to the Church in which she lived; it was a relation that involved her self-effacement, almost like disappearing, as she became transparent enough to expose the mysteries of salvation to which she was dedicated. In this self-effacement, in this transparency, the Founder saw the best means of depicting the attitude of an apostle in a world caught up in religious crisis but not to be moved toward God by any external force. The behavior suggested by Father Colin in his famous "unknown and hidden" is accordingly saturated with the Marian presence, which accepts a non-prominent role and which moves the Marist less to focus on her than on Christ and the Church, and to keep self out of sight while serving the Church. Mary's role comes down to establishing the approach to life that was hers, without having attention constantly focused on herself.

The Place of Mary among Marists

The spirit of Marists is the spirit of Mary because of the special relationship existing between her and them, a relationship established, from Mary's side, by a gratuitous, gracious choice, by the gift of her name, and, from the side of the Marist, by the acknowledgement of her as mother, model and superior. This means making the spirit of Mary one's own, being imbued with her way of being and acting, in somewhat the same way as one might be influenced by a spiritual guide.

Fr. Colin insisted a great deal on the ties between Mary and the congregation. She is its foundress and gave it its name, making it, with a gracious choosing of its members, her own family; she thus creates between them and herself a sort of pact from which springs the duty to behave as her true daughters and sons, reproducing in the Church the mystery of the hiddenness and efficacy of her life. What is brought out is the consciousness the social body must have of its responsibility to a person, Mary. Coste concludes:

> Understanding of the Marian mystery as the mystery of the hidden life and reflection on the pattern of a Marist's responsibility, on his way of living and acting, are for Father Colin one and the same thing. We may say that this was his only insight, but he certainly pushed it to its utter limits.

Basic Orientation of the Lay Marists

Here is how Colin's idea of the Marist spirit was expressed in a statement intended directly for lay people:

Mary has chosen Marists, who bear her name, to be part of her family. They relate to her as to a person whom they admire; they try to adopt her attitudes of simplicity, familial love, and mercy. Whatever they notice in her, they try to weave into all their actions.

The basic orientation is to the person of Mary as the one who most surely leads to God, the model of a simple and unostentatious way of attending to what needs doing. Mary's name, Mary's spirit, and "the work of Mary" grip the minds and hearts of the people who look upon Mary as the mother of all Christians, the gate of heaven, the mother of mercy.

They are grateful to this mother by whose intercession "every excellent and perfect gift from above descends upon each one from the Father of lights." They are grateful that she guides them on the way that leads to the lasting presence of God, that is, to salvation.

Loving her as children love their mother, they speak to her in prayer. They believe that she cannot forget her children but hears their prayers and requests and perceives their needs. They believe that she is open to all miseries and devoted to relieving them.

The Marist Way and Mission

The reality conceived of as Marian and lived as such may be expressed in phrases like the following: service without notice, doing what others won't do or can't do, the primacy of living over talk, availability for collaboration with others, a simple and warm approach to people, a certain aptitude for working without too much insistence on personal success or consolation. These values are passed on by a tradition in which the Marist of today is conscious of sharing.

Marists throw open these values to others, invite them to share in a climate of life, to take on the Marist identity; but this happens only when personal witness and communication have made it possible for others to see this spirit, this climate, as a reality. This is one of the reasons why lay Marists would form a group: to be a school for the spirit by which people gradually become "the work of Mary."

In the long name Colin gave to the lay branch, "Confraternity or Association under the Auspices of the Blessed Virgin Mary for the Conversion of Sinners and the Perseverance of the Faithful," it is plain to see that Marists are committed to working not only for their own salvation but for that of all people. They are concerned that those alienated from God might turn to God and that those who have come to know God might persevere in loving and living for God. The Church's call for the evangelization of people who are far from God mirrors the existing consciousness of Marists and heightens their awareness of a need to which they are basically dedicated. Thus, their personal quest for holiness is paired with the mission of helping other people to find God, embrace God, and practice their religion.

In all they do, Marists are primarily conscious of who they are — family members who belong to a loving Mother. And so they focus on thinking, feeling, and acting in the spirit of Mary. What Marists do — the great variety of ways in which they contribute to evangelizing and saving the world — will be explored in the second part of this book. They are characterized, however, not by *what* they do, but by the *way* they do things, by their spirit.

Unworthy, Imperfect People Graciously Chosen

When, in October 1993, an invitation was given to people in Marconia, Italy, to become Marists, one man said it sounded very lofty and concluded, "I'm not worthy." He was right, of course. No one is "worthy" to be chosen by Mary as one of her own; she chooses imperfect people. (The man in question must have come to understand this because, two days later, he had overcome his hesitations and, along with twenty-some other people, pledged himself as a Marist.)

Indeed, Marists include imperfect people who are searching for God, for faith, for meaning in their lives, as well as other imperfect people whose faith keeps growing stronger. Marist lay groups are not formed by an elite but are places where people whose faith is not well formed and who have more questions than answers can let their hair down and be helped to search. Those who have begun to relate to Mary (to "think as Mary, judge as Mary, feel and act as Mary") are also searchers, people who ask, like Mary, "How can this be?" (Lk 1: 34). The Marist way is for young people in their uncertainties and for older folk who have learned to recognize their imperfection. It is not for those belligerent "righteous" people whose attitudes and actions often defile the image of God as benevolent creator and of Mary as mother of mercy.

Images

Medieval knights and nobles had the heraldry of their shields; modern business corporations carefully design their logos. A graphic image is easily recognized and remembered and can say much about an individual or a group. Three images for the Marist family or the lay branch in particular — and one of

Mary as Mother of Mercy — deserve mention here, even though they are only indirectly related to the Marist spirit.

A Tree with Its Branches

A tree with its branches, as we saw above in chapter 1 (*pp. 2-3*), was taken quite early as a symbol or emblem of the Society of Mary as initially envisioned with its three or four — and eventually five — branches, one of which, from the very beginning, was composed mainly of lay people.

In speaking of the various "branches" of the Marist project, it was only natural to think of a tree with its branches, probably by analogy with the biblical image of the vine and its branches. Its basic significance is that of a spiritual unity in a common spirit without which nothing worthwhile can be accomplished. While the image of a multi-branched tree never stood for one congregation from which the others branched off, it may have at first represented a juridically unified Marist Society unified under a single Superior General, but it did not do so after 1835 when it became apparent that the original plan for such a union would not be sanctioned by the Holy See, and certainly not after 1842 when a final attempt at the unification of the branches was not approved. We may, however, look upon the tree (or trunk) as a fitting symbol for the unifying and animating spirit drawn from Mary and the intuitions which she inspired.

The tree with its branches thus aptly represents the closeness of the Marist laity and the various Marist religious congregations and their spiritual unity in the Marist spirit.

A Barque or Small Sailing Ship

The image of a barque or small sailing ship was used on several different occasions, generally in reference to the Society of Mary and sometimes to the lay branch. In 1852, Julien Eymard used the image of a small boat, a "skiff" (*nacelle*), for the Third Order of Mary (of which he had been director until the year before); it would "safely pass through storms and tempests ... toward its beloved port," even though it might be shaken by a "fickle and relentless wave."

Among the spiritual experiences of the lay Marist, Marie Elisabeth Blot, was one which occurred in May 1866, around the feast of Pentecost, when she saw the Society of Mary as a small barque, and later when she saw what she understood to be the barque of Mary, aboard which all members of the Society were in safety. Colin took up the same image in May and August 1873 in writing and speaking of the Marist Society as the barque built and piloted by Mary; it would save from eternal shipwreck those who got on board and stayed there in the spirit of Mary and under her guidance; it is like Noah's barque (the ark). A preliminary draft of the foreword to the Constitutions of the lay confraternity says that "this Association is like Mary's little ship (*navicula*), by means of which all Tertiaries can safely cross over the dangers of the sea which is this world and can more securely reach the port of blessed eternity."

A Bridge

The image of the bridge, presented above in the foreword (*pp. v-vi*), is a fitting image for the apostolic, evangelizing mission of the Marist laity.

The Virgin Mary Wearing a Mantle

Connected with spreading the Marist spirit all over the world, with the ideal of making the whole world Marist, there is the image of Mary with a large mantle covering and protecting all humanity. This basic representation, which admits many variations in its details, features a gigantic-sized Mary wearing on her shoulders a mantle or cloak, the lower folds of which are extended on either side of her (and held open either by her extended arms or by hovering angels); sheltered beneath the folds of the cloak is a crowd of smaller-sized figures representing all the faithful (or, at times, a particular city or religious order or family). In a scholarly study of this iconographic theme, Jean Delumeau traces it to the ancient Byzantine East and describes its spread throughout western Europe in the Middle Ages, noting a decline in its popularity with the Renaissance. In all forms of the image, Mary is seen as the Mother of Mercy, the Mother of all, sheltering the people, protecting them against plague, famine, and war, understood as punishments coming from the justice of God.

Colin could have come upon such an image of Mary in many different places in his travels in France and Italy; there is a representation of the theme in the large mural on the north transept wall of the Belley cathedral. He brought the image into his talk to the Fathers at the end of their retreat in 1844, when he said that we should be grateful to Mary "for having chosen us to spread her Society, this Society comprising the three branches, because Mary intends to cover the whole earth with her mantle. Let us make this lovable mother known, let us bring people to love her. Let us win hearts for her. In winning them for Mary, we win them for Jesus." Here, alongside the image of the Society with its branches, Colin reinforces the ideal of the "whole world Marist" with a reference to the image of Mary covering the whole world with her mantle or cloak. Denis Maîtrepierre used the same image in 1853 when he wrote: "Isn't the Society like the mantle of the Blessed Virgin which offers shelter to all God's children? And aren't the four branches like avenues which lead us beneath the folds of that protecting mantle?" Still later, in 1919, when Alphonse Cozon was commenting on the provision in the lay confraternity's Constitutions that all Catholics could be admitted, he wrote: "if the royal mantle of that august sovereign is immense and ought to serve as refuge for all without exception, as has been prefigured, according to the holy fathers of the Church itself, by Noah's ark, the refuge of all the elect, it follows that the Society of Mary ought to be open in a certain way to all people and it ought to consider itself as contributing to the salvation of all."

While Colin retains the idea of the Mother of Mercy protecting all people, the mantle also takes on the notion of a gathering of all people by being linked with the ideal of "the whole world Marist."

Themes Studied in a Course for Lay Marists

A course on certain themes of the Marist spirit was given in 1992-93 in two places in Ireland: at Mount St. Mary's, Milltown, Dublin, and in Dundalk. The remainder of the present chapter is the text from this course; it was worked out in Milltown by two lay Marists, Breda McGee and Anne Hynes, with Marist Fathers Gerry Kane and Martin McAnaney; coordinators of the course in Dundalk were Eileen McCann, a lay Marist, and Marist Father Luke Monahan, who is co-animator of the Marist laity in Ireland.

The material used in these courses is presented here for two reasons: (1) it can enrich any reader with its contemporary reflections on aspects of the Marist spirit, and (2) it can serve as a model for the study of the Marist spirit and mission by groups in other countries.

Gracious Choice

What is particular about the Marists? What makes them tick? To understand the particular way that Marists seek to live the Gospel is not easy. It takes time. It means coming back to the same words and phrases over and over again. Each time you come back to them, you begin to understand them a little more deeply, especially in what they mean for you. These words and phrases have a deep meaning for Marists. They are symbols that are rooted deep in Marist history. "Gracious choice" is one of these phrases.

However, in another way it is easy to describe what Marists do and how they try and live. They see themselves as being chosen by Mary (gracious choice) to bear her name, and to do her work. Her work involves reaching out to those who are trying to live the Gospel in a secular world, helping them to persevere. It also involves reaching out to those who claim to have "lost the faith," those who find their faith has no particular impact on their lives. Marists try to reach out to people in the very same way that Mary herself would. In other words, gently, simply, with a maternal concern for them.

Can anyone be a Marist? Obviously this is not a way of life that is restricted to priests or brothers or sisters. In fact, if it is to make sense at all, it should be open to everybody in the Church, not just those who have a particular vocation to religious life. So parents can be Marists, teachers can be Marists, school-children can be Marists (even if they are not in Marist schools), single people and married can be Marists. In fact the whole world can be Marist. Marists must include everyone, no matter what their standing or role in life.

From this point of view, lay people are simply more numerous than priests, brothers and sisters put together. They are therefore more available to so many, particularly to those who have been hurt by the Church, those who feel alienated, and those who are suspicious of official Church figures. If Mary is to reach out to everybody, it will be through the whole Church, and not just one small section of it. Through laity in particular, Mary's gracious choice will embrace the whole world.

Is it, then, simply a matter of deciding that I want to be a Marist and calling myself one? No, it is not quite that simple. Remember "gracious choice." It may seem that you have made all your own choices in life; it may seem to be purely a coincidence that you heard about Marists in the first place. Maybe it was an accident that you simply ended up in a Marist school, or a Marist parish, or met some Marist that you admired and were attracted to in some way. But Marists understand (eventually) that in fact it is they who have been chosen. Sometimes it only gradually dawns on them, after they have been living as Marists for years. In fact when they come back to the phrase again, it often has a deeper layer of meaning. None of us can assume that we fully understand it.

In one sense we can say exactly what it means: we have been chosen to do Mary's work, and to live the way that she did. But it takes a long time to actually experience what that means, and not just know it in our heads. No amount of reading history or delving into abstract tomes can make up for personal reflection on the simple themes. In fact it involves more than just reflection. It is living and moving inside this understanding of life, allowing your own life story and the sense of "gracious choice" to influence each other.

So everyone can be a Marist then? Yes, but it may not be to everyone's liking. Not every member of the teaching staff in a Marist school will feel the desire to find out more about it. Not every parishioner in a Marist parish will want to know more. Not every pupil in a Marist school will feel any attraction for the Marists or even be curious about what motivates or drives them. Some may even be hostile towards Marists. We are all broken people, and through our personal weaknesses, we may hurt one another. So some people will be committed, others simply curious, and others bored. This is where "gracious choice" comes in.

Who does the choosing? From my viewpoint, it may seem that all the choices I make in life are my own. It is I who choose certain careers, or certain places to worship. Other times I don't have choices. My parents sent me to a particular school, or the Marists ended up taking over the parish where I lived for years; or there was a job available in a Marist school when I went looking for one. But other points of view exist. As Marists, we believe that Mary has chosen us to bear her name and do her work. So it is Mary who does the choosing.

What then do we mean by "gracious"? By "gracious" we mean that it is, somehow or other, one of the ways in which God's love for people is made real. In other words, perhaps it is only through me that God may be able to reach out to certain individuals, and then only if I relate to them in the way that Mary herself would, were she in my shoes.

It also means (and this is the deeper sense of the word) that it is "gracious" for me. In other words, it is not simply a job that I am given to do; it is much more than that. It is the way that God has chosen for me. It is not primarily about the work that I can do, my skills or ability or talents. It is about me in all my weakness and brokenness. I have been chosen to be a Marist, not because I am better than others, but simply because it is part of God's mysterious plan for my life. It is the way in which God's grace comes to me. That is what we mean by "gracious."

What will be asked of me if I say "yes" to this "gracious choice"? And how much time will that involve? If you say "yes" to a gracious choice of Mary's, you can be fairly certain that whatever is asked of you will be no more than you can give. And being of Mary, it will be asked gently. In the first instance, you may simply be asked to get used to the idea of doing Mary's work, of thinking like her, judging like her, feeling like her, and acting like her.

On a more practical level, being a Marist is not like being attached to any other religious order. In fact it is not about being attached to a religious order at all. It is being part of a way of living, a spiritual movement. So you can be as much a part of it as anyone else. You have a right to be. You will not be working for priests, or brothers, or sisters. It may be better to think of working with them rather than for them. And indeed, as a Marist, you may also be working independently of them, especially when the religious aren't around. How much time will it take? That is up to the individual. In one sense it is not a valid question; a way of living takes up all your time.

Why should I feel chosen by Mary? What particular "work" of hers could I possibly do? Ultimately that question can only be answered by individuals in the silence of their own hearts. This sense of "gracious choice" may take some time to develop. It is not an attractive idea to everyone. For many it can be gradual, a sense that develops over time. A lot will depend on your own circumstances. It could be something as simple as relating to other people, even members of one's own family, the way Mary herself would relate to them.

It all sounds so "holy." We live in a very secular culture, where living a life of faith is difficult at the best of times. We need all the help we can get. But we need to stop thinking of life in terms of some activities being holy and others being not holy. Our ordinary day's activity is ultimately holy work. Thirty years of carpentry in the life of Jesus was holy work. Similarly, the work we do, the people we influence in our daily lives, the way we relate to each other — all of that is holy work, though it may feel ever so ordinary. It all depends on your vantage point. From God's point of view the connections are obvious.

Where does the phrase "gracious choice" come from? Perhaps it is good to share a little of our history. The Marists were founded in France in the last century. Perhaps the three most significant people involved were Jean-Claude Colin, Jeanne-Marie Chavoin, and Marcellin Champagnat. They are the ones who founded the Marist Fathers, Sisters and Brothers, respectively. The sense of being chosen graciously for a special task had been with them since the very beginning. However, it wasn't until 1868 that it was first written down in the words we know — "gracious choice."

Why is it so significant for Marists? By the time the phrase "gracious choice" was written down, it represented the fruit of a life-long reflection on what it meant to be a Marist. It was based on the lived experience of the early Marists, the Founders. They had struggled with the first inspiration. They tried to find out exactly what being chosen to do this work meant. The phrase "gracious choice" summed up for them one aspect of what their lives were about.

So this "gracious choice" reminds us that we are part of something that is far bigger than ourselves. Something that stretches right back through history to the time when the whole thing began. So being a Marist is not simply a personal choice we make. It is not simply for our own good. It reminds us that we are part of a living tradition. We are invited, as Marists, to share in that tradition, to live that experience ourselves. So everything we are involved in, every school, every work, is part of a long tradition and a long history. Every time we hear the phrase we are reminded of who we are, what we have to do, and what an honor it is to be part of it. That is why it is so significant.

One recent Marist writer, Fr. Frank McKay, put it like this: "We believe Colin and his companions, both men and women, were chosen by Mary to have a special relationship with her and to allow her to continue her work through them. They had a strong sense of personal destiny. They knew they were called to be something and to do something; to a special way of living and to a special purpose for living. In other words they received through Mary a spirituality and a mission. By a spirituality is meant simply the way we relate to God, to ourselves, to our neighbour and to the world. It is the way we try to live the Gospel. Like the first Marists we believe 'we are the bearers of a particular grace in the Church and for the Church. We do not hide it under a bushel, we wish to share it.'"

How can I take this further? How do I find out if I am "graciously chosen"? It is really only through reflection by individuals, through discussion and over time, that a sense of "gracious choice" will emerge. There is something about people coming together to discuss their own insights, and share the events that throw light on this for them, that is much better than simply reading documents such as this. This may help, but that is all it can do.

It may be a useful exercise, particularly if you are a member of a group, to try and tell your story from a Marist point of view. If you are not a member of a group, you can always write your own story. What would your own "Marist story" be? At what stages in your life was Mary significant for you? How did you come to this stage, of actually reading this particular document? Is there any sense of a guiding hand behind the random events of your life? And what about your home life? Is your life simply an accident? Have you ended up this way just through random choice? Or is there a deeper meaning?

In the world of today it is difficult for many to have faith. Some people in their mysterious journey through life sense, only dimly at first, an invitation to share particularly in Mary's concern for humanity and to share her work. This is at the root of being a Marist. By living your daily life in the spirit of this gentle woman, you are responding to an invitation of God and an invitation of Mary. If you can say "yes", in however mysterious a way, to this invitation, then she gives you her name and you are Marist. A gracious choice indeed.

"I was the support of the new-born Church; I shall be also at the end of time."

One of the phrases that guided the early Marists was: "I was the support of the new-born Church; I shall be also at the end of time." This phrase was important because it came as a revelation. So it wasn't just somebody's bright idea. It was divinely inspired. It gave them a sense of what Mary's work is, and what they were asked to do. To put it bluntly, their mission, their task was to allow Mary to support the Church through them just as she supported the early Church. The same is true for us today.

So Marists want to keep things the way they are? No, far from it. If the Church today is in need of change, then Marists have a role to play in it. The sort of Church we want is like the newborn Church. Let's look at the first part of the phrase: "I was the support of the new-born Church." What image comes to mind when you think of the Church? Do you think of a building? Or priests and bishops? Or a group you are involved with? We all have a sense of what the Church is. And that affects the way we live our faith.

Some people see it as an **institution**. This tends to be a safe place, where deep values are cherished, where there is a rock-like security in a time of huge change. But now the institutional Church is seen by some to be out of touch, dominated by celibate men, using the traditional image of Mary to keep women down, reluctant to change, serving its own interests.

Others see the Church as a **community** gathered around Jesus Christ. It is warm and inviting, and open to everyone, a place where people feel they belong. It is personal. However, there is also a danger here, that we will forget about others. All groups have a tendency to close in on themselves. We settle for what we know, stop inviting the stranger, and simply enjoy being around the fire ourselves. (Is this true for your group, if you are part of one?)

As Marists, we are trying to build a Church **like the early Church**, where everyone is "of one heart and one mind," a community. That is what seems to be lacking nowadays. In our big churches, it is hard to get a sense of community. Whenever people feel they belong, it is normally in small groups. Sunday mornings in parishes just can't seem to provide that.

How do we know what the newborn Church was like? We look at Scripture. The Acts of the Apostles gives us a picture of the early Church:

> From the Mount of Olives, as it is called, they went back to Jerusalem, a short distance away, no more than a sabbath walk; and when they reached the city they went to the upper room where they were staying; there were Peter and John, James and Andrew, Philip and Thomas, Bartholomew and Matthew, James son of Alphaeus and Simon the Zealot, and Jude son of James. All these joined in continuous prayer, together with several women, including Mary, the mother of Jesus, and with his brothers. (Acts 1: 12-14)
>
> The whole group of believers was united, heart and soul; no one claimed for his own use anything that he had, as everything they owned was held in common. The apostles continued to testify to the resurrection of the Lord Jesus with great power, and they were all given great respect. None of their members was ever in want, as all those who owned land or houses would sell them, and bring the money from them, to present it to the apostles; it was then distributed to any members who might be in need. (Acts 4: 32-35)

We know that Mary was there. (Maybe that's all we know about her. Maybe that's all we need to know.) We know that they were a strong community, open to outsiders. And we know that they developed structures — how else would they manage to distribute their goods?

However, much of what it means is left to our imagination. Maybe that is why it is so fruitful for Marists. It is a useful exercise to let your imagination wander into that upper room, to sense what was really happening. What sort of a community was it? What exactly did Mary do? What way did she support them? How did they organize themselves? Who went out to preach? (Why not try this in prayer?)

Fr. Colin once said, "We must re-create the faith of the first believers. That is precisely what was foretold in our earliest days. It was foretold that the Society of Mary was to take as a model none of the congregations which preceded it; no, nothing of all that; but that our model, our only model, was to be and indeed was the early Church. And the blessed Virgin, who did such great things then, will do even greater ones at the end of time, because the human race will be even more ill."

Does this mean that we are to re-create the past? No, that would be a mistake. Fr. Colin also said, "The Society must begin a new Church over again. I do not mean that in a literal sense, that would be blasphemy. But still, in a certain sense, yes, we must begin a new Church." This is the Church Marists are trying to build — a Church with the face of Mary.

In the phrase we are looking at, Mary reveals that her way of being in the early Church was as a **support**. What that means is that she exercised her leadership in a supportive way, not seeking the limelight. Mary saw to it that her Son was proclaimed, not herself. It is a type of leadership that is strong and subtle at the same time, never getting in the way, but being quietly assertive, almost in the background. Yet she had a central role to play.

But what about the Church today? That brings us to the second part of the phrase we are looking at: "I was the support of the newborn Church; I will be so again at the end of time." Mary's influence didn't end in the early Church. She promised that she would be the support of the Church at the end of time just as she was in the beginning.

How? In many different ways. But one important way is through the people who bear her name, through Marists. This is where we come in. We have the same concerns as Mary. It is up to each of us in our own situation to see what that means in practice. For instance, it might pose questions about how we are involved in our own parish.

What do you mean by "end of time"? The "end of time" is a technical phrase, one that speaks of the world today. It is a way of understanding the times in which we live, an invitation not to get settled in, but to feel all the instability and insecurity that there is at the moment. There is an urgency about it all. Many people do settle in and drift along on the tide. Marists are asked not to, but to face the deeper questions.

Why did it take 1800 years before a group emerged with the actual name of Mary? Why did nobody think of that before? Or to put it another way, why did God, or Mary herself, wait until now? In a mysterious way it means we are part of this "end of time." Mary has been a persistent phenomenon in the Church from the very beginning. Why is that?

Could we lose sight of Jesus by concentrating so much on Mary? Only if we concentrate on Mary in the wrong way. There are some groups who devote themselves to Mary, and Jesus rarely gets mentioned. Marists are not like that. The attitude Marists have is the same as Mary herself — that it is Christ who should be proclaimed, not Mary. We can learn from her how to say "Yes" to God completely. There are two other Marist phrases that we will come to that help to explain it. The Marist Brothers in particular have a motto, "All to Jesus through Mary." Again the Marist Sisters draw great inspiration from the phrase "Think like Mary, judge like Mary, feel like Mary, act like Mary in all things." If we lose sight of why we do this, then we could go astray. But then we would stop being Marist.

What has that got to do with me? Well, it means that if the image of Mary in the newborn Church fires me in some way, then I can see how I would fit into the Church of today. Whatever I am involved in, a parish, a school, or raising a family, could be the birth of something new.

In the early days, this phrase prompted different reactions. Some Marists concentrated on how it affected their daily lives —

the values of simplicity, obedience and patient hidden work. Others were fired by the urgency of the task. Still others were attracted by the notion of Mary's constant presence and activity. And some began to get a sense of what a new Church would be like. Which of these makes sense to you? Or is there something else?

For instance, there is a lot of talk here about the Church. Where is your faith nourished? What is your experience of your own parish? How could you change things? More importantly, how could you change things the way Mary would? How will you find out what Mary would do?

It will take time for the sense of this Marist thing to develop. We can't rush it. Sometimes it may feel as if things are out of focus. It may be very vague, and full of questions. If so, just let them be. The reason for this is that because it is up to you to find out how to put it into practice. No one can tell you precisely what to do. The example Mary gave us is 'pondering.' She "treasured all these things, and pondered them in her heart" (Luke 2: 19). The best way to become a Marist, to deepen the sense of mystery that is at the heart of our lives, is to ponder.

Hidden and Unknown in This World

Now for something practical! Another phrase that Marists use regularly is "hidden and unknown in this world" ("unknown and indeed even hidden in this world"). It describes the way Mary was present among the Apostles. It is also the way that Marists try to be present today: quiet and unassuming, taking a low-profile approach. It affects the way we think, the way we behave, and the way we relate to others, at home or at work.

What does it mean in practice? Fr. Colin once said "When God speaks to a soul, he says many things in few words. So it is with the saying 'Hidden and unknown in this world.'" There is a wealth of meaning in these few words. We might be inclined to laugh at the idea — imagining Marists disappearing into a closet, or having a handy excuse to hide away. It may seem pretty powerless. It may be off-putting. It may even feel like a barrier to actually doing something. But it is not. It is about how we act, not whether we act. It needs to seep gently into our consciousness, affecting everything we do, freeing our own spirit, and opening us up to God. We can see what it really means by looking to the person of Mary.

"Hidden and unknown in this world" describes beautifully the way of Mary. She never pushed herself forward, or demanded her rights.... The conception of Jesus must have been one of the most hidden moments in human history.... She gave birth to Christ in a stable, hidden from so many, unknown to so many.... They lived unnoticed for thirty years as an ordinary family in Nazareth.... She followed her Son discreetly, as part of the crowd.... Through her prayer she did more.... She was a leader in the early Church. But she was not the figurehead — she could probably do more good by remaining hidden and unknown in this world. There is more than one way to exercise leadership.

Is it relevant to the way we live today? We live in a time of great change. It is particularly difficult for lay people in the Church. There are many good people who want to be actively involved in their own local parish, and yet they experience a Church that doesn't seem to care about them. So many of them tend to find a place where their own personal needs for support are met. They find (or form) some group where they can belong, and express their faith. But there are others out there who have not had the same opportunities as they. They too are searching. They may not be ready or even willing to become involved with a Church group. Who will be concerned for them?

"Most unbelievers today are not convinced and militant atheists. They are the nice couple next door who just don't know" (Snijders, p. 106). They will not want to talk to priests and religious whom they regard as "professionals." Who, then, will reach out to them? This is one place where being hidden and unknown is so important. Lay Marists can be a non-threatening presence, someone with whom they can open discussion, without feeling brow-beaten or overpowered.

Can you give an example? We all know some people who are approachable, and some who send out signals that they don't want to be disturbed. It is often an unconscious thing. Yet one of the greatest needs in the world at the moment is the need for people to listen — to take time for others. We live very busy lives, and we don't give people what they need most — time.

If we are hidden and unknown, we forget about ourselves, our own interests, our own concerns, and we become more available to others. We can really listen, because our minds are not full of our own needs and wants. A mother, no matter how she is feeling, is always there for her children, and concerned for them. At times she transcends herself. It is the same for us. "Hidden and unknown in this world" will encourage us to become aware of other peoples' needs and less concerned about our own. We will not be tempted to give advice, or be over-anxious about what to say. We will simply listen. Often that is all people need — a listening ear. They will solve their own problems most of the time, if they meet someone who is gentle, attentive, present, just like Mary. There is a deep joy in being able to help someone else.

It sounds very simple. Yes, it is. Simplicity is the key. But "hidden and unknown in this world" is also a very effective way of influencing a group. There are many different ways of doing this. Some people do everything themselves. Others need to be in the limelight — so that everyone knows they are important. Others lead by example. Some exert their influence by encouraging, some by talking loudly, some by demanding, some by bullying, some by issuing rules to be obeyed, and some by being hidden and unknown. Look at the drama of the wedding feast of Cana (John 2: 1-10). Mary is there ... they need wine ... she notices their need ... she tells Jesus ... she advises them what to do... Jesus acts ... the crisis is over. As Marists, we notice the needs of others ... we are discreet ... conscious of a personal relationship with Jesus, we act ... and the new wine is theirs. We meet people at the point of their need, and lead them on from there, gently and without intruding. And when it is over, we slip quietly into the background.

To act like this means that nobody will be left out, nobody will feel threatened, nobody will react to the person concerned, because he or she does not get in the way. There will be space for everyone to express themselves. The centre stage will always be free since nobody is hogging the limelight. This is true for families as well as larger groups.

Marist laity in particular are asked to be the heart and mind of Mary for our world. To go places where clergy and religious cannot go — even in their neighbourhood; to go and gather others. They are not asked necessarily to teach or preach, but simply to gather. "The spirit of 'hidden and unknown in this world' leads Marists to embrace a life of simplicity, modesty, humility. Nothing in their personal life or behaviour, neither pride nor personal ambition, will cause people to resist the salvation offered them by God. Like Mary they are to be gentle with others, respectful of their freedom, and sensitive to their point of view. In this spirit they are able to hear the longings of the people of God and discern the signs of hope present in today's world" (Const. SM 1987, no. 24). We try to show that in a harsh world of unbelief, faith is still possible — faith in a God who is compassion and mercy. We do this in the way Mary has shown us — in a hidden and unknown way.

What about prayer? Being a Christian today is a hard struggle. The world doesn't seem to want to know. Yet, we find God important in our lives, and we search for a sense of that hidden reality. Being "hidden and unknown in this world," keeping a low profile, could also be a description of how God is present in our world. Being hidden can be a gentle lesson in how to help others in their desire for God. God never forces anyone. Neither do we.

Yes, we pray. We pray hard, for others as well as for ourselves. Fr. Colin said "Prayer is the means of doing good while remaining unknown... The blessed Virgin made no stir, but she prayed a lot." But we don't force our way on them. We hold this truth — that Jesus was born, that he died, and that he is risen. And we stand beside others in their unbelief; not preaching at them, but standing with them, humbly, simply and with compassion. And we walk with them as they discover these truths for themselves.

"Hidden and unknown in this world" is not just a technique, no matter how effective it might be. We imitate the person of Mary — not a method. We have been given her name, and it is by becoming more like her that we truly become all that God wants for us.

The wisdom of this way of being grows as we ourselves grow spiritually. The way to do this is to practice it in our daily lives, in the small encounters that make up every ordinary day. For many people that is what conversion means — it is a slow gentle process. Like Mary, we ponder "hidden and unknown in this world." The phrase lingers in our minds, and over time it reaches deeper levels within us. Others will notice the change, particularly in our own homes. So many people fight endless battles at home, trying to change others' behaviour. We change what we can — our own behaviour, and we allow others to respond to that change, in their own time and their own way.

"Hidden and unknown in this world" also tells us more about the type of Church that we want to build — a Church that is discreet, and attentive to the profound changes that are happening; a Church that is not self-centred, but concerned about peoples' real struggles; a Church that is merciful, pointing towards a gentle God, a God who often remains hidden; a God who is revealed in the most unexpected of places. We want a Church with the face of Mary. Such a Church is born in our hearts as we become more like Mary ourselves; as we begin to think like her, feel like her, judge like her and act like her in all things. That is how such a Church and such a world is born.

"Think as Mary, judge as Mary, feel and act as Mary in all things."

Here is another phrase that shows us how to be Marist in practice. Once again it has deep roots in our history. It was finally expressed in this form in the later stage of Fr. Colin's work on the constitutions of the Sisters and Fathers. It tells us how deeply we need to identify with Mary, if we are to bear her name and do her work. In a sense we have to become Mary in the world today. In other words, it is more than looking to Mary and being inspired by her way of life. It is much deeper.

If Mary is to support the Church today just as she supported the early Church, one of the ways she will achieve this is through us. If a new Church is to emerge, then it is up to us to build it; not according to our own designs and plans. That will always be a temptation — that we simply follow our own personal project. Instead we have been given designs — and plans. Our way of building this new Church is by thinking like Mary, judging like Mary, feeling like her, and acting like her in all things.

"Thinking like Mary" — how could we do that? In any situation, before we react, we can ask ourselves "What would Mary think about this? What would her concerns be?" Obviously this would influence our thinking. It might prompt us to remember aspects of the situation that would not be our own way of thinking. We can reflect on aspects of the Gospel stories about Mary. We can also ask her to guide us in our thinking and acting. Even the very fact that we stop and think will influence us. Often in difficult situations our first instinct is to react rather than respond. And our reaction may not be the best. But if we train ourselves, as Marists, to stop and think like Mary, then our response will be different.

But surely it is impossible to feel what another person feels? Feelings are personal. We are not asked to give up our own personal feelings. That would be impossible. But very often something happens and we have conflicting feelings about it. For example, I am watching television news about a tragic famine. I may feel guilty — I am well-fed. I may feel powerless — what can I do? I may feel angry — why doesn't somebody do something? All these emotions and more will come instantly. But I may also feel moved with compassion for these people. That is more than an emotional reaction. That is different from guilt or anger or feeling useless. It has more to do with others than with myself. It is a concern for others, something that draws me out from myself and helps me grow spiritually. I have some control over this type of feeling, this sort of response. That is something I can learn. If I settle for the emotions of guilt, anger, powerlessness, I may just switch channels, and think that there is nothing I can do. Soon, I will become dulled and blunted to the pain of others. But if instead I respond to the feeling of compassion, or mercy, then I remain very much alive, even if there is still nothing I can do about it. If I were to ask myself: "What would Mary, the Mother of Mercy, feel about this? What does Mary feel about this?" — then there is little danger that I will grow dull and blunted.

So we are to try and imitate Mary, then? It is much deeper than that. If we try to imitate Mary, it may be too much to ask. We may always be conscious of our own shortcomings. We may easily become discouraged. We may add to the burden of false guilt that afflicts so many of us. Also, there is nothing concrete given here. How, for example, are we to imitate Mary in all our actions? What were her actions? Too much is left to our own imagination. If we strive after such an impossible ideal, which is far beyond us, we will soon give up. We will think that this ideal of being Marist is very nice, but really it is beyond me, and must be meant for better people. That is not what Mary would want. Being Marist is open to everybody.

Mary lived a very simple life. There were no great acts, nothing beyond us. No great deeds or powerful stances. Instead there was a daily faithfulness, a daily care. She lived moment to moment in the presence of God. She was very familiar with God. Indeed as the mother of Jesus, many of his qualities would have been her qualities. We are all shaped by our parents, and often turn out like them in ways. So too with Jesus. Mary's greatness was in her simplicity, her ordinariness. She showed that the little moments of our lives are important to God. Thinking like Mary is allowing God to be the focus of our lives, the centre. None of that is beyond any of us.

If we don't imitate Mary, what then does it mean? As Marists we are not being invited to follow a new role model. Instead we are invited to refer to a person. This is an important distinction. We are conscious that we are chosen to bear the name of Mary. So we refer all decisions to her. Faced with a decision, we do not try to imitate what she did. Instead we ask ourselves: "What would she think of it, how would she judge, how would she feel about it, and finally what would she do?" It is an intimate relationship, not just imitation of a role model. At a superficial level, this relationship may not make sense. But at a spiritual level, it does. It opens us up to the Spirit of God, just as Mary was open to the Holy Spirit at the Annunciation. She teaches us how to be as open as she was, and this is what God asks of us.

If we try to imagine Mary in a modern setting, faced with modern problems, we may go astray. It is better to develop a relationship with her, to meditate on Mary in the Gospel, to pray to her as Mother of God, seeking her guidance. This will give us a spiritual awareness of Mary, which will gently influence our lives. **Mary is not a role model we struggle to imitate; she is a living person with whom we have a special bond.** This has a profound yet gentle influence on our lives. It does not abuse our freedom, or force us in any way. That would not be Mary's way, or God's either. Remaining close to her, we become like her, and her way of following Jesus becomes our way.

Surely a special bond with Jesus is enough? This is the aim of every Christian. It is the purpose of our lives, to give glory to God by having the same mind as Christ. But there is more than one way to cement this bond. Any person who helps us forge a stronger bond with Jesus is helpful. For instance, the disciples once told Jesus they tried to stop someone who was using his name to cast out devils. Jesus told them "Anyone who is not against us is for us" (Mark 9:38-40). So if a relationship with Mary draws us towards God, so much the better.

Now **that** is what being Marist is all about: having a relationship with Mary that draws us closer to God. This thought will not please everyone, only those who are attracted to the Marist way, and are experiencing her influence in their lives. Remember the element of gracious choice. But for those who are Marist, called according to the mysterious plan of God, it is the best way, perhaps the only way, for them. As Marists we live the Christian life in the unique way she did during her life on earth. In this way we co-operate with God's design for our lives. It is almost as if God sees that we need to be coaxed gently, and Mary is the person, the instrument used to coax us.

These Marist phrases will not mean much to us unless we know Mary as a person. But if we do know her, then the pieces of the jigsaw begin to fit together. We keep Jesus Christ at the centre of our lives. But as Marists, we know Mary as a person. We have a relationship with her, and this is an important influence in our lives. We find that Mary is somehow there in the picture as well, in the background. If we try to concentrate on her, she will probably slip quietly into the background again, and Jesus remains at the centre.

Occasionally we will sense echoes of Mary in other Marists. It is very subtle, but we may catch the signs. It is something about the way they relate to other people, something about the way they work, something about the way they are. It almost feels as if Mary is present somehow. But it is God who is uppermost in our minds — not Mary. That is the effect of thinking like Mary, judging, feeling and acting like her. Perhaps the best way to understand this idea is to live with it for a while. Develop a relationship with Mary, and judge it all by its fruit — does this relationship with Mary lead you towards God, or away from God?

Chapter 4
Lay People in the Church

Your experience?

You have your own story to tell about how you have experienced the Church. Perhaps it is happy story: the Church has been a place where you have found God and his love. Perhaps it is a very sad one of a place where you experienced rejection or pain. Perhaps you are rather content with the way things are. Perhaps you are very impatient for change which you see coming all too slowly, if at all. Whatever the case may be it is through the Church that we come into contact with Jesus and become his disciples. Marists belong to the Church, to the People of God — in its weaknesses and strengths. To be a Marist is to be part of the Church, to share its life and to try to bring a certain quality of Mary's presence to give it a more human and gentle face — a Marian face.

Awake to a Call

In this chapter we want to look a little at the Church in relation to lay people. The Church, like the society around it, is in a stage of great transition and change. Part of this change is undoubtedly an awakening by the Holy Spirit of a sleeping giant. There has been a sleeping giant in the Church. This sleeping giant consists of the greater part of the People of God — lay people. This giant has been awakening during the past few years, and it is the hope of Marists that it will do so even more in the coming decades. More and more lay people are becoming aware of their rights and responsibilities as disciples of Christ in the Christian community. Attitudes are changing and there is the dawning realization that all the members of the Church have the "right to full participation in the Church's life and responsibility for its mission" (John Jago, S.M., *Mary, Mother of Our Hope*, p. 27). However to enter into this, inspired by Mary at Nazareth and in the midst of the Apostles, is to be a Marist.

Something to Work From

A Synod on the laity was held in 1987, and its results were put together by Pope John Paul II in a document called *The Vocation and Mission of the Laity* (30 December 1988), which is very rich and can serve as a basis for our reflections. A renewed role for lay people is happening out of a renewed understanding of the Church. To make this vision a reality in the daily life of the Church is not easy. There are great tensions and pain involved in the changes required. There is no way these growing pains can be avoided. It is often difficult for clergy to let go of a tight control, to share in partnership with people and to take risks. They can feel insecure in this new situation. Often lay people feel that they are not welcome or that they are inadequate. Nevertheless there is a power of renewal at work that will surely continue to grow slowly despite setbacks. Let us have a look at something of such a vision of a Church where lay people have a full place.

An Image — the Vine

How we have come to know Christ and to follow him is unique for each of us. The moment when we received the sacrament of baptism in the Church was the moment when we became Christians and we implicitly received an invitation to share personally in the life of Christ — to follow him as friends and disciples. Jesus usually spoke in images to communicate his message, and one image he used helps us to grasp something of the meaning of this at a deep level. He said, "I am the vine, you are the branches. Whoever remains in me, with me in him/her, bears fruit in plenty" (Jn 15: 5). Here Jesus compares himself to the vine which has sap and life, and he tells us that when we are bonded to him (by faith and baptism) we are like living branches of the vine and our lives will be fruitful in virtues and good deeds. Our life experience as Christians may have had lots of ups and downs, with times of darkness, doubt and struggle or even distance from Christ. We may not have had any real experience of the love of Christ for many years of our life, but behind everything the call of Christ in our baptism was always there.

Into the Heart of God's Love

If we develop an adult faith in Christ, we come to know the enormous love God has for us, and are drawn into a new life in God. St. Paul puts it beautifully: "Blessed be God ... he chose us in Christ, before the world was made, to be holy and blameless, and to live through love in his presence" (Eph 1: 3, 4). So the Church in its innermost heart is really the place where God most shares his life and love with us. Our Creator and Lord offers us himself in intimacy through Christ in the Church. As an institution the Church has its weakness, but it is also where God's glory is revealed and where his love can be known and accepted.

A Mystery of Love for All

At a deep level the life of faith in Christ draws us into the depths of the mysterious God and his incredible love. In so far as the Church is where this happens to us, it is called a *mystery*. Mystery: a somewhat technical word to get at the fact that the Church is more than a human institution. It is where the God of mystery comes close to us in a special way through his word and sacraments. It is important to note that everyone who is baptized is invited by Christ to come to know and live as fully as possible God's great love. This means that there is a fundamental equality among all believers. This means that all are equally members of the Church; all are called by Christ to take seriously their invitation to live fully the Christian life. "All baptized in Christ, you have clothed yourselves in Christ, and there are no more distinctions between Jew and Greek, slave and free, male and female, but all are one in Christ Jesus" (Gal 3, 28). All baptized people share the same dignity, being reborn into the life of God as disciples of Christ and united in the People of God. In daily life in the Church, the dignity of all is not always recognized, and the destructive power of division and discrimination weakens considerably the realization of the unity we should all have in Christ. To be a Marist is to be a creator of unity and to do all in a merciful loving way, even though painful confrontations are sometimes necessary.

Lay Persons

So the basic invitation to be fully Christian is common to all baptized people. However, within this fundamental call, individuals have different roles. Some receive the sacrament of Holy Orders and some join religious congregations. However, most Christians are not called to be priests or religious, but they have their own calling in the world. It is not a question of one being loved more by God or the other being of lesser importance but rather of each one responding to God's unique plan for him or her. We are in a partnership with one another. (*On the terms, "lay" and "laity," also see above, pp. 5-6.*)

A New Life

Before thinking about the practical things of living as a lay Christian in the Church, it is good to explore briefly the great dignity of a Christian. The sacrament of baptism really gives the seed of a new life — a seed that should develop by a life of faith. The gift of God in baptism is a spiritual rebirth which makes the Christian a child of God in a new way. St. Luke tells us about the voice of God which said at Jesus' baptism: "You are my beloved Son; with you I am well pleased." We too need to hear in the depths of ourselves the same truth, "You are my beloved son/ daughter; with you I am well pleased." To hear in ourselves that same great truth needs a certain attitude of openness and inner listening to the word of God. Mary is an excellent example of this and Marists follow her attitudes of finding the presence of God in their experiences. It is important to note that being a child of God has nothing to do with childishness and can never be an excuse for immaturity or a flight from responsibility. Rather it has to do with recognizing that we are now reborn of a free loving

God who invites us to an inner spiritual freedom which leads to a fuller human maturity.

One Body in Christ

In a mysterious way baptism also brings a real incorporation into the crucified and glorious body of Christ. This may sound very abstract, but in fact it is very real. We become sisters and brothers of Christ in the one new family. This is an invitation to die to sin with Jesus and to live a new life with him in a bond of love with others. "We, though many, are one body in Christ" (Rom 12: 5). To have an intimate relationship with Christ is an invitation he gives to all. This is intensely personal but not individualistic, as we are only united to Christ in so far as we are really part of his people, part of his Body. This involves the Church in a real challenge today where it seems to be so difficult to create communities in parishes. Many Christians do not find a real expression of this where they live. Marists too are challenged to be agents for bringing this about. We remember that Jean-Claude Colin was very fond of the phrase from the Acts of the Apostles "one heart and one mind." To be a Marist in the Church is to work to bring about a "new Church" — where there is a welcome for all, a sense of belonging, and a real solidarity.

Given the Holy Spirit

All Christians receive the Spirit of God to make them holy and to equip them to share in the mission of Jesus as the Saviour-Messiah. We usually associate the word *holy* with the saints in heaven or people who are exceptionally close to God here on earth. But in the early days of the Church a common way to talk about the members of the Church was *the holy ones* (*the saints*). It was one of St. Paul's favorite ways of addressing them. This did not mean that they were all perfect or living the Christian life to a high degree. It meant rather that the *Holy* Spirit lived in them and worked through them. The Holy Spirit gave them a share in the holiness of God. The same Spirit of holiness is present and working in all Christians today who are alive to God. This activity of the Spirit makes us share in the mission of Jesus.

The Mission of Jesus

God loves tenderly as a mother the world he made. We know Jesus was sent to draw the world back to him. This work of Jesus can be put under three headings. He was Priest, Prophet and King. His work of restoring all creation to God will not be finished until the end of time, and he wants his Church — and each member of it — to share in this mission.

Lay Faithful and the Priestly Mission

In his role as priest, Jesus offered himself on the cross and renews this in the Eucharist for the glory of God and the salvation of the world. A Christian lives an ordinary daily life — of prayer, family and work concerns, relaxing, experiencing hardships, etc. — but if these activities are carried out in the Spirit, they become spiritual sacrifices acceptable to God through Jesus Christ, and are of great value in his eyes, especially when there is great love behind them. All this is celebrated and offered to God in the Eucharist along with the Lord's Body. This living through love in the presence of God in all the human realities of life brings the lay person to holiness and builds up the Reign of God. The image of the vine and the branches can help us to grasp this also.

Lay Faithful and the Prophetic Mission

Jesus, in the witness of his life and in his words, proclaimed the Reign of God. Without becoming preachers or full-time workers in the Church, all lay people in their own way share in this. The present-day lay Christian knows his/her responsibility for mission. He/she sees this not simply in terms of helping the hierarchy but seeks to do this with a certain autonomy knowing that Christ entrusted his mission to all God's People — of which the lay faithful make up the overwhelming large part. Often it will be just by the unassuming quality of a loving and responsible life. However, the committed Christian is on the lookout for occasions of announcing Christ by word, either to unbelievers to draw them towards the faith, or to the faithful to instruct them, strengthen them, incite them to a more fervent life; "for Christ's love urges us on" (2 Cor 5: 14). (Vatican II, *On the Apostolate of the Laity*, no. 6). The Holy Spirit gives special graces (charisms) for this prophetic sharing in Christ's mission and people have a right and duty to use them. Often lay people feel a sense of inadequacy because of a lack of training and so on. Special training is not needed to deal with many ordinary situations. But it is wonderful to note that today many lay people are taking courses and studying how to live their Christian faith in a way that really touches their daily lives and touches others as well as transforms society. It is clear too that the situation of many lay people in the world of today calls for strong words and actions for justice.

Lay Faithful and the Kingly Mission

In his life Jesus was totally faithful to God's will, and wanted to bring the world back to that will. The Reign of God was arriving with him but will not fully come until the end of time. Christians are asked to work for that coming — for the spread of the Reign of God. First this takes place for each one in his/her own life by the spiritual combat against one's own sin and sinful tendencies, and then in the gift of oneself to serve Jesus present in others, especially the poor and neglected. In a particular way lay people are involved in drawing creation in its different aspects to the genuine well-being of humanity. No part of the world or humanity is outside the range of this.

The Secular Character of Lay Life

The Church is present in this world and is concerned that all things be renewed in Christ. It is particularly here that the role of the lay person is important. Most people live in the circumstances of an ordinary life — family, work, friends, study — or poverty, unemployment, family difficulties, illness. It is precisely in these circumstances that they are called by God to fulfill his plan for themselves and for the world. By living the new life of Christ in these situations and in the world of politics, economics and culture they find their vocation. This is the secular character of the lay vocation. It is worth remembering here the images of Jesus, "You are the salt of the earth. ... You are the light of the world" (Mt 5: 13, 14).

Holiness

The prime and fundamental vocation that God assigns to each person who is baptized is the vocation to holiness, that is, the perfection of Christian love. God wants all to grow in divine love — in fact, all are invited and bound to pursue holiness and the perfect fulfillment of their own state in life. This is not just a question of good morals, but has to do with our deepest identity. Christians, reclothed in Christ, and living in the Holy Spirit, radiate something of the holiness of God to others. It cannot be denied that this is a great struggle at times, and that growth can be slow or even reversed. But the Lord is always present to help, and we have Jesus, Mary and the saints as models who followed their call to holiness in a thorough way.

Life according to the Holy Spirit

It is well worth quoting and pondering a paragraph from the synodal document on laity: "Life according to the Spirit, whose fruit is holiness (cf. Rom 6: 22; Gal 5: 22), stirs up every baptized person and requires each to follow and imitate Jesus Christ in:

- embracing the Beatitudes,
- listening to and meditating on the Word of God,
- conscious and active participation in the liturgical and sacramental life of the Church,
- personal prayer, in family or community,
- the hunger and thirst for justice,
- the practice of the commandment of love in all circumstances of life,

- service to the brothers and sisters, especially the least, the poor and the suffering."

This is a prayerful and faith-filled life, but it is a life of involvement in the world. There is great variety in the way this happens for different people.

In Unity with One Another

All that has been said above could be put under the heading of the lay person's sharing in the Church as *mystery*. But the Church is also a *communion*. To see what this might mean, we can return to the image of the living vine. We are the branches of the vine in union with Christ. Being joined to Christ in this way we are in union with one another. Bonded to him, we are also bonded to each other. God does not save us and bring us close to his love merely as individuals but as members of one Body, as a People, as the family of God united in the Holy Spirit, whom Jesus gives us and who dwells in each one of us. This must be expressed in loving relationships between us.

Gifts and Tasks from the Spirit

As well as making us one, the Holy Spirit is active in giving ministries, gifts and tasks to different people to make the Church grow and be alive, as well as to extend the Reign of Christ for the salvation of the whole world. These gifts and ministries are not just given to a select few. Every Christian has her/his role to play, though each in a different way. Some lay people feel they are not "holy" enough for all this, or that such things are only for priests and religious. Some priests, too, are very reluctant to let lay people exercise their gifts. Such attitudes can block the Holy Spirit. At this present time the Holy Spirit seems to be calling the whole Church to recognize and encourage the place lay people have in using the gifts and exercising the ministries that will enrich God's people.

For Service

These gifts and ministries are given to be used in a spirit of service, in the way Jesus served like a good Shepherd, and in the way Mary selflessly and lovingly gave herself to sharing in the plan of God. They should not be seen as a way of gaining status or used for selfish interests. A deepening spirituality ensures that they result in the unity and growth intended by the Spirit.

Ordained Ministers to Encourage All

The ordained members of the Church — who are only a tiny proportion of the People of God — have a particular role to play in serving the Church and saving the world. But their role is only one among many, and pastors should acknowledge and foster the ministries and gifts and role of all Christians. The various roles need not be confused. The sacrament of baptism gives everyone a place. It gives everyone the responsibility to evangelize. There is also the work of guiding and service that comes from the sacrament of Holy Orders. As mentioned above, there is often a tension here as lay people now wish to take their full and proper place in the life of the Church and can blocked by narrow clergy reluctant to let go of a tight control. The human weaknesses also of fear, power struggling, jealousies, etc., can frustrate progress and cooperation. These negative things can come from all directions in the Church and to overcome them understanding, respect and humility are needed.

Universal and Local Church

The Church is universal — spread out over the world. But it is also local — in each diocese. We live our life at the level of diocese and parish, but it is necessary to have a catholic spirit, aware of belonging to the world-wide People of God, which is often in great need. The Spirit of God invites us to think and act at this wider level too.

The Parish

Parishes are usually big and impersonal. Yet people are looking for community and friendship. To make the parish more like the family of God as a fellowship filled with the Spirit calls for the talents and energy of lay people. The task seems too big. In order that parishes can really become more like communities of Christians, there should be an adaptation of parish structures to promote the participation of the lay faithful in pastoral responsibilities. In fact, the canon law of the Church allows great flexibility here. Another way to foster church fellowship is the development of small or basic communities where people can share the word of God and express it in service. Such communities can be centers of spreading the gospel. There are many movements within the Church that enrich the Christian community, and they give scope for lay initiative. However sometimes these can be divisive and narrow. When lay Marists group together it should be always with an eye to the unity of the parish.

Communion Leads to Mission

Living a life of holiness and sharing together in the local church — *communion* — leads us to spread the Reign of God — *mission.* Jesus sends his Church to continue his mission of salvation (*see also above, pp. 89-90*). The words of Mark's gospel still resound in our ears, "Go into all the world and preach the gospel to the whole creation" (Mk 16: 15). It is customary to call this great work *evangelization*, and it is very much at the heart of what the Church is called to be and do. Effectively bringing the love of Christ and extending the Reign of God is essential to the life of the Church.

Evangelizes All

The Lord himself entrusts a great part of the responsibility for evangelization to the lay faithful. An awakening to become a disciple of Christ, who calls each by name, leads to a desire to play a part in evangelization. In other words, lay people who share in the *mystery* of the Church, and in the *communion* of the Church will sense the desire to share in the *mission* of the Church. They have the right and duty to do so. This sharing in the work of evangelization is by no means the sole preserve of the clergy and of those other laity who are vowed religious.

A Time for Re-Evangelization

Whole countries and nations where the Christian life was formerly flourishing now experience increasing indifference to religion. Many live as if God did not exist. In many countries millions are forced to live below their dignity as human beings. Peace between people is constantly being threatened. Our world risks ecological disaster. Millions have never heard the call and message of Christ. These situations cry out for the mercy and healing of God. The hour has come for a re-evangelization.

The First Step

The synod, in its analysis of all this, suggests that the first step is for the Church to do something to "remake the fabric of the ecclesial community itself." In other words we begin with the Church becoming more faithful to the message of Christ, and one of the keys to this is the lay faithful. Lay people, who know in themselves how to overcome the separation between the gospel and life, who are fearless in their adherence to Christ, will bring a shining and convincing testimony: "Each Christian's words and life must make this proclamation resound: God loves you, Christ came for you, Christ is for you 'the Way, the Truth and the Life' (Jn 14: 6)." For many people the lay Christian may be the only gospel, or good news, they will ever meet.

Go into the Whole World

There are millions who do not know Christ their Redeemer. Some lay people are willing to leave familiar surroundings at least for a time to go to places of mission. Married couples, in imitation of Aquila and Priscilla (cf. Acts 18; Rom 16: 3) are offering a living witness to the love of Christ in mission territories. There are many possibilities for lay persons' involvement in enriching the Church's reaching out. Lay Christians from older churches long established can help in younger churches and *vice versa*. There is an important place for the activities of lay people in inter-religious dialogue, especially in fostering mutual respect and diminishing prejudice.

The Church — Servant of All

Part of the mission of the Church is to be of service to the human person and to society. The dignity of the human person is very great, and this demands the respect, defense and promotion of the rights of each one. In so many ways today this dignity is not respected. There are gross violations of human rights: e.g. the unborn killed; populations deprived of housing, work, adequate food; atrocities of war. There are new challenges brought by technology, biological and medical science, etc. There are serious moral issues behind all this, and lay people can have a great influence in the task of calling culture back to be genuinely human.

Service to Society — The Family

The first expression of the social dimension of the person is the family. This partnership between man and woman is the first form of communion among persons. The lay person's duty to society begins with the family. As the basic cell of society, the family is meant to be the cradle of life and love. Human egoism, totalitarian politics, poverty, etc., can work to destroy this community, and so the Church, particularly through its lay people, has an important role here..

Service to Society — Justice and Charity

Jesus came to serve and not to be served, and to give his life (cf. Mk 10: 45). Down the ages the Church has engaged in works of mercy to the poor, ill, aged, and those in any kind of need. Lay Christians have given a shining witness to their love of Christ by caring for him in the least and most vulnerable. This charity is the soul of solidarity. In many places state agencies have taken over the care of people's needs, but there is still place for personal Christian love. The blatant injustices in the world call for a response from those who care as Christians.

Service to Society — Public Life

Justice and the common good can never be separated from a love that serves the human person. The lay person has influence here in promoting these in public life — in economic, social, legislative, administrative and cultural areas. Charges of careerism, corruption, self-interest that are often directed against those in politics do not justify the absence of Christians from public life. Lay people with a real Christian spirit can bring into the public eye a concern for the common good and for the rights of the weaker sections of the community. These times require solidarity — seen as the firm and persevering determination to seek the good of each and the good of all in local and international life. Lay people in the world can be justice-seekers and peace-makers.

Young People

Young people are both a challenge and a hope for the Church. The relation of young people to the Church varies very much from place in the world at present — from a rejection of or indifference to the Church to a firm commitment to its mission. Whatever the case, the Church has much to talk about with youth, and youth have much to share with the Church. They are not just the object of pastoral concern, but rather they are to be encouraged to share their faith and work for renewal of society.

It is interesting to note an increase in the number of young people who want to live a Marist life.

Children

Children are the object of the Lord Jesus' tender and generous love. They are a symbol of the spiritual qualities needed for entry into the Reign of God. They remind us that the missionary fruitfulness of the Church has its basis not in human means and merits, but in the free gift of God. The lives of innocent children, who sometime experience great suffering, are a source of spiritual enrichment for us.

Older People and the Gift of Wisdom

The Bible sees the older person as a symbol of someone rich in wisdom and the fear of the Lord (cf. Sir 25: 4-6). The elderly can be witnesses to the tradition of the faith, teachers of the lessons of life, and workers of charity. Their contribution is valuable to the Church, and their role does not stop because they get older but rather deepens as they grow spiritually.

Women

There is an increasing awareness of the dignity and role of women in the Church. They were very active in the ministry of Jesus and in the early years of the Church, and we see their involvement in many ways today. There are real and painful tensions as the Church comes to a newer understanding of the role of women and expands the range of their ministry and participation.

Men

The coordinated presence of both men and women in the saving mission of the Church is to be encouraged to make the mission of the Church richer, more complete and more harmonious. Men have their own contribution to make, but sometimes they abdicate their Christian responsibilities, particularly in liturgical participation, catechesis of their own children, and other religious activities. Responsible men with a Christian spirit can have an exceptional influence in society.

The Sick and Suffering

Even a partial list of those ill and suffering in serious ways is long — the sick, the disabled, the poor, migrants, prisoners, refugees, the unemployed, abandoned children, the lonely elderly, victims of violence. The Church presents a Messiah whose suffering led to a new life. The Church itself often suffers and the suffering of its members is part of its suffering. It labors to relieve human misery where it can. Where nothing may seem possible to change a painful situation it offers the figure of Jesus the Redeemer. He invites all to unite their suffering with his and to receive his risen power in themselves and share it with others. Lay people who are blessed with health and freedom can help those suffering in many ways and in so doing express their participation in the work of Jesus.

Maturation

To return to the image of the vine and branches again — the branches can grow or wither. Their vitality depends on their remaining attached to the vine, which is Jesus Christ. "He/She who abides in me and I in her/him bears much fruit, for apart from me you can do nothing" (Jn 15: 5). There is a dialogue between God and the Christian. To know God's love is to know a constant invitation to grow. So, rightly, greater Christian maturity is sought by many of the lay faithful today who do not want to be treated as immature children, or as second-class members of the People of God.

Discovery of One's Vocation

The goal of this growth and development is the ever clearer discovery of one's vocation and the ever greater willingness to live it so as to fulfill one's mission. To be able to discover the actual will of the Lord in our lives involves the following:

- a receptive listening to the Word of God and the Church,
- fervent and constant prayer,
- recourse to a spiritual guide,
- a faithful discernment of one's gifts and talents,
- as well as attention to the social and historic situation in which one lives.

Living One's Vocation

Of course it is not simply a question of knowing what God wants, but of doing it, and developing the capability to respond more freely in cooperation with grace. Saint Leo the Great says: "The one who confers the dignity will give the strength!" This living of one's vocation is not just a "spiritual" activity but embraces the whole of a person's life in the world. There can easily be a split between a person's faith and his/her daily life. Religion can be compartmentalized, and its influence may not enter into the attitudes and values that one has in dealing with the business of life. This is a particular problem of our time.

Aspects of Formation

To enable us to live our faith in an integrated way, an integrated formation is necessary. It includes the following elements:

- spiritual formation which leads to an intimate union with Christ, fidelity to the will of God, and devotion to others in charity and justice.
- doctrinal formation which gives a better understanding of the faith, and its relations to the world of today.

- formation in the Church's social doctrine, particularly as so many lay people are actively involved in the problems of the world.
- formation in human values.

A Total Formation

God's work in forming his people is revealed and fulfilled in Jesus Christ, the Teacher who reaches into the depths of each one's heart through the living presence of the Spirit. Nothing can replace this inner formation coming from the Spirit of God. The Church, too, is called to take part in the divine work of formation — by sharing its life, teaching and actions. This involves the Pope, the diocese, the parish and smaller church communities. The Christian family as the "domestic church" is the natural and fundamental environment for formation in the faith. Schools, movements and associations also help in this task. The formation process should pay special attention to the insights and experience of the poor. If the gospel is to be a living word, local cultures should be respected, particularly minority groups in large nations.

The Future

The vine will continue to grow and its branches bear fruit. At this particular moment in the life of the Church, it seems that its future vitality will come largely from the lay faithful. Those who are sensitive to the call of Christ and give themselves generously, like Mary, to the following of the Lord will hasten his Reign of justice and peace and love. Your Reign come, O Lord! Mary, Mother of the Church, intercede for us!

Part 2
Doing the Work of Mary

Chapter 5
Membership, Structures, and Practices — Basic Points

Creative Fidelity

Building a bridge between being and doing is the core of fidelity, that fidelity which Gabriel Marcel terms "the exact opposite of inert conformism" and which for him implies an active and continuous struggle against hardening into habit. For Marcel, fidelity is "a mysterious incitement to create."

Not surprisingly did Fr. Bernard Ryan, a former superior general of the Marist Fathers, take up the term *creative fidelity* to speak of what we need to be and to do. In being truly faithful to the Marist spirit, we will certainly create ways of doing and associating that meet the needs of our time and local cultures. Though using a ready-made blueprint seems easier than drawing a new design, the new wine should probably not be put into the old wineskins.

There is a creative power in a tradition to which we strive to be faithful. We find that fidelity to a tradition gives us a creativity which far surpasses any creativity we would have were we to start from scratch rather than work out of a tradition. The question is not whether it is legitimate to change things, but to see how fidelity to Mary and the Marist foundation incites us to create new forms, etc.

The present chapter suggests a few basic points to keep in mind; the following two chapters give examples of application. These points are meant only as a help to the resourcefulness of those who want to make the whole world Marist.

Becoming a Marist

People react differently when they first hear of the ideal of making "the whole world Marist." Some smile and think "What a nice idea!" but draw a blank when it comes to action. Some simply dismiss the idea as a pipe dream not to be mentioned too often. Some think of recruitment schemes and the formalities of enrollment. Each of these perceptions, however, falls short of the Marist founders' "all-encompassing vision." The name Marist, we have seen, is derived from the name "Mary," and so the creative fidelity about which we are speaking means first of all being faithful to Mary. The very name carries us beyond organization and procedure. In other words, there are many ways of being faithful to Mary:

(1) Colin, in speaking to the Fathers' "chapter" or policy-making meeting of 1866, put it most broadly when he said that people "are all Marists insofar as they are working for the good of the Church." He was telling his audience not to be jealous of the good which others were doing but to rejoice in it; anyone can be "Mary's" in this broadest sense.

(2) Still in broad terms, we have those who have come under the influence of Marists in some way and have absorbed certain Marist values perhaps without even knowing it.

(3) There are also those who admire certain things about the Society and would like to be associated with it. But they do not wish to make any kind of commitment. They do not belong to a group as such, nor do they wish to be called Marist.

(4) Finally, we meet various kinds of people who do want to be called Marist and to live by the Marist spirit the best they can.

With them it is no longer a question of degree or intensity; they are all fully Marist. It is in regard to them that we now consider the question of membership in the Marist family.

Who may become a member? From 1833 to 1874, Colin maintained: "All who have the use of reason may enter this Association, whatever their condition, whether they be men or women, whether they be among the faithful or among sinners, so long as ... they hold to and profess the faith and teaching of the Roman Church, whole and complete." Sectarian clashes in the nineteenth century kept Colin and others from conceiving of the possibility of the Marist spirit reaching believers beyond the Roman communion; in the light of ecumenism, however, we do not hesitate to welcome all whose who come to adopt the Marist way.

A lay person might well ask, "*How do I become a Marist?*" There are different answers insofar as there are different ways of "adhering to" Mary, of being part of the Marist family, though all are equally valid. Essentially, *one becomes a Marist by some contact with another Marist and then identifying with the basics of the Marist spirit* — with its reference to Mary herself, to the intuitions of Colin as founder, and to the living tradition experienced by the social body of Marists (*see p. 57; also pp. 66-67*). The basics are indeed simple, though the spirit is rich enough to keep one going and growing a whole life long.

The formalities of admission can vary, or there may be no formalities at all. Early and late in his life, Colin said that membership came with the inscription of a person's name in a list of members, but even this is not absolutely essential.

A good example of an absence of formality is the case cited by Frank McKay of "the young Filipino girl whom one of our missionaries met on his first visit into the mountains of Mindanao. When he introduced himself as a Marist priest, she replied: 'I'm a Marist, too. Quite a few of us around here are Marists.' She and her friends had been introduced to the Third Order when an earlier Marist missionary had visited. They knew what they were and the way she and her friends wanted to live."

Some groups have a formal admission ceremony in which the new member declares before the group his/her desire to be a Marist and is admitted by someone holding responsibility in the group. Some token, such as a medal, may be bestowed on the new member. It may happen, too, that formal admission as a Marist is preceded by an initiation period during which the prospective member is given instructions in the Marist spirit and in the practices and rules observed in the group. Variations on the above procedure may occur when a person is received individually rather than into an established group.

Colin's 1874 Constitutions provided for a kind of special membership in the Association for "participants" who are "admitted into a sharing in its prayers and merits. In this way, there may be included any sinners, even the most incorrigible, as well as children who have not yet reached the age of reason and even those still in their mothers' wombs, etc." The enrollment of unborn children, with the proviso that the Marist group will pray for them, is described below in chapter 6.

Any kind of payment of money at one's admission is absolutely forbidden by Colin and the whole Marist tradition. A group is allowed to take up a collection "for the payment of necessary expenses," but no one is ever to "ask for anything for the exercise of the sacred ministry."

In different cultures and periods of history, various groups may want more or less formality in admission or none at all. Whatever is done, it should be kept simple and all monetary consideration should be avoided.

Structures and Rules

"Keep it simple" summarizes Colin's approach to structures and rules for the lay branch. In 1838, in fact, he envisioned no rule at all for most lay Marists but only a few suggested pious practices; for a sub-division of those who wanted a stricter, more retired lifestyle, there could be a short rule of life.

The 1874 Constitutions for the confraternity give a broad outline of orientation and simple practice. Colin was an idealist, one who inspired, a prophet. He did not set down details for the function of local groups. While this may be disconcerting to those who seek a blueprint for action, it also means that Marists are free from preordained patterns. Colin asked for fidelity to the name and the spirit of Mary and seems to expect his disciples to use not a little creativity.

Some groups last only a short while; others may continue for a long time. It does not matter, as long as "some good is done," as Colin would put it. Some, like the Marist fraternity of catechists which existed in Paris in the early twentieth century (*see pp. 167-168*), may get absorbed into something bigger.

Local Leadership

Colin's plan for the lay branch of the Society of Mary is not detailed. He said that the particulars should be left up to the "local directors" to meet local needs. Originally, the "director" of a particular group would be a priest; Colin preferred that this would normally be a diocesan priest, the pastor of the local parish, but, as things developed, it was often a Marist priest. In any case, Marist religious or priests have a non-directive role. According to the Colinian ideal, they should be "servants, not masters." They should want to be helpful, not in charge. In doing so, great humility and abnegation is needed. Keeping the membership lists, though of secondary importance, could be seen as part of the task of promoting unity in heart and mind. Marist religious and priests are also expected to give retreats and other kinds of instruction on the Marist spirit and spirituality — without charge. We recall the specific injunctions not to use the Marist laity for financial gain.

With the strong urging of official Church teaching, as we noted above in the foreword and chapters 1 and 4, lay people have come to assume their rightful place in leadership roles. A priest or a Marist religious (Sister, Brother, or Father) may serve as a spiritual guide and advisor, but lay Marists are not mere followers (except of Mary herself): the leaders come from the lay Marists themselves. Indeed, lay leadership is called for by the fact that, in the Marist family, this is a distinct branch which "should shine out into the Church" according to the Colinian ideal. No longer does a group have to wither if a priest is not there to preside at meetings; the lay leaders now preside, set their agenda, and carry it out themselves.

Practices

The basic practice of Marists is prayer, without which any activity is like casting seed on barren rock or a beaten path. At the same time, they know that authentic religious experience, in which the ordinary response is prayer, must be integrated into everyday life. So it is that Marists are particularly concerned about those who have never been part of the fold and those who have strayed. Their sense of mission leads them to make their prayer's primary intention: that those alienated from God might turn to God and that those who have come to know God might persevere in loving and living for God. Prayer underlies and accompanies whatever Marists do to spread the word of salvation. Colin urged: "The Society of Mary desires that we, her children, should be missionaries of action and missionaries of prayer."

Prayer, like everything else, should be kept simple; extraordinary or sensational piety is to be avoided. What Colin recommends — and sometimes calls "the Christian's religious exercises" — is simply the ordinary prayer of any practicing Christian. Mental prayer is also recommended, but in the simple form of thinking about God, Mary, and religion; for this, reading from the Bible or a religious book usually helps. Whatever forms of prayer individual Marists may use, these may include — but are not limited to — the recitation of formal Marian prayers. If Marist groups adopt any devotional practices, they should follow Colin's advice to keep them short, simple, and easy to do.

Apostolate and Evangelization

Since their earliest days Marists have been aware that a world without God is empty and desolate; they have responded to irreligion with a missionary dynamism. While conducting missions in the rugged Bugey hills of France, Marists asked people to pray for the conversion of sinners and the perseverance of the faithful. In this particular instance, the faithful were those who had been converted during the parish mission just conducted. The Society grew up in a missionary situation, and these early beginnings have colored its entire attitude and spirit.

The lay branch of the Society shares the same outward movement. It is not essentially contemplative in the sense of centering solely upon the relationship of its members to God but — because the authentic test of belief is in what we do — extends its reach to the world. It shares the sentiment of Charles Péguy, who asked: "What will the Lord say if we go to him without all the others?"

The first group of lay Marists in Lyons, France, had an energetic apostolate; this group of young men (the Tertiary Brothers of Mary) started a Catholic school, visited the poor in their homes, hospitals, hospices and prisons, taught catechism, and sought to involve other people in their good works. In 1840, a women's group of lay Marists saw themselves as "apostles to their relatives and friends, in the whole city"; they were "silent apostles" through prayer and good example.

Though we know that it is the task of the laity to evangelize the world, many (Marists included) "leave it to the priests and the religious," as the layman Kevin Luxford has said, "because we may often feel so inadequate; yet we share the missionary responsibility." He adds: "Marist Laity can give us the training and the prayer formation that will enable us to fulfill our vocation as the People of God. I think that with evangelization it is important to make a start, even though what we do is very small. As we do, we will grow and develop enough to meet the more difficult situations that may lie ahead."

The lay Marist usually lives with her/his family, so it is natural to emphasize engaging in the works of one's local parish and actively cooperating with one's parish priests. The need of the Church — normally the local Church — is a good criterion for concentrating one's attention. Doing in a quiet, unassuming way what needs to be done to draw people to God and the practice of the faith, lay Marists do not draw away from local works but enhance them. By carrying out the role proper to the laity in the Church, these Marists work in partnership with the local clergy and not at cross purposes with them. Usually, this means bringing the Marist spirit and constant dedication to already-existing organized efforts and sharing that Marist spirit with those attracted by it. Some groups of lay Marists, however, have a more specifically missionary, evangelizing aim, moving and acting in the low-key Marist way to help the unchurched find God in the practice of religion.

Variety of Organizational Structures

"The community of believers were of one heart and one mind" (Acts 4:32). This mind-set characterizes lay Marists, as indeed all members of the Marist family. This meant — and still means — unity between the various branches of the Marist laity in the recognition of a common spirit and a common purpose in the midst of a broad spectrum of specific orientations and modes of living. Not only that, but "one heart and one mind" also indicates a sense of unity with the local church.

Colin envisioned a wide variety of people involved and in the types of involvement. In his mind, there could be different groupings of men and women, children, young adults, and those of a more mature age. A few groups would be like what we now call a secular institute, with some even living in community, while the usual pattern would be that of people simply living at home and gathering periodically to pray and draw inspiration from the Marist spirit.

The multiplicity of branches among the Marist laity is the complement of their unity. It may be a problem if it causes confusion; it certainly is a problem wherever jealousy or mistrust occurs between various groupings or wherever someone doubts the authenticity of ways other than what one is following. Yet, a great number of forms is at the same time a prophetic sign. Colin insisted to Cozon that the unity of lay Marists lies in the name and spirit of Mary and not in the uniformity of structure or practice. The only telling objection Colin had to Eymard's Third Order was that it was "too circumscribed." (While this assessment may seem too simplistic, a critical examination of the record confirms that Colin commended Eymard for all the good he did but objected to the latter's narrow concentration on a pious elite; Colin wanted something broader, extending to the whole world.) Vigorous measures are needed to foster the many diverse approaches to making the whole world Marist, to heeding the needs of both the Church and the world of unbelief. Two subpoints:

(1) Strong affirmation can be given to every kind of grouping that embraces the Marist spirit, to those who cling to the ways they knew forty years ago as to those who take untried steps in conversion and perseverance. And this applies not only to the attitudes of Marist religious but perhaps even more so to the various groupings of associated Marist lay people. Among Marists, there are no "second-class citizens," no ranking of more perfect or less perfect types of organization. All Marists do well to offer more positive signs of confirming each other in both their diversity and their unity.

(2) There are already effective new ways in which the mission of the Marist laity takes shape in today's world. Examples: in one part of the world, a Third Order comes alive among a sizable expatriate population and engages in apostolates that include door-to-door evangelization; in another part of the world, Marist lay missionaries are organized to work in places where it would be unsafe for priests to enter; in yet another country, support-groups are formed for young mothers; yet again, university students as Marists persevere in the faith and spread it. Some groups model their structure on that of Base Christian

Communities or of the Focolare movement; some offer Marist spirituality to those completing the rite of Christian initiation to help them to stay together in faith-sharing after baptism. The following chapter gives specific examples of what people are doing nowadays: these are intended as models of what is possible. In addition to the examples given in this book, the further sharing of testimony and information — through existing periodical publications and other means of communication — will help in stimulating and promoting the creativity needed.

Chapter 6
Contemporary Models of Organization and Action

For someone to live the Marist spirit, groups and organizations are not necessary, yet for most people they are the best means of learning and sharing about the Marist way. The possibilities are endless in number when it comes to such organizations. In what follows we give a brief description of some of the ways which are being used at the present moment in the Marist world to help make the Marist way of life a reality for many people in different parts of the globe.

Some developments in the Marist Way in England, where Fr. Michael Coleman, S.M., is the animator.

In 1989 the title Marist Way was adopted for all the groups of Marist lay people.

One very effective way of sharing Marist spirituality in England is by the newsletter, a regular monthly publication which contains an explanation of some aspect of Marist spirituality as well as news. Every month 1500 copies are distributed. It is distributed in several parishes where there is no formal Marist Way and the priests are quite happy with the response.

Fr. Coleman visits the groups and individuals who show an interest. He also conducts a number of pilgrimages every year and takes this opportunity to introduce people to the Marist Way. Pilgrimages are also organized to the "Marist places," i.e. the places in the area of Lyons in France where the Marist project was born. This kind of experience helps to develop the Marist spirit in the pilgrims.

It should be said that the expansion of the Marist Way in England is due in no small measure to the Marist Sisters.

There is a card available which gives a very brief exposition of the Marist Way, along with a simple suggested spiritual programme:

To say some short prayer to the Mother of God at the beginning and end of each day.

In popular use are the three "Hail Mary's" together with the prayer: "We Fly to Your Protection."

To spend some time each day, if possible, in quiet personal prayer to Jesus Christ.

(Reading and reflection on the Scriptures can be of great help to you in your prayer. This kind of prayer is a source of spiritual gifts from God.)

To make a brief examination of your conscience at night, thanking God for His goodness to you and asking forgiveness for your failures.

To offer a decade of the Rosary daily, for the conversion of sinners. (This intention is particularly close to the heart of Mary, Mother of Mercy.)

Sr. Shirley Day, S.M., working in El Placer, near Palmira, Colombia, gives the following information.

In 1989 Fr. Bernardo Escobar invited us to begin a youth group in his parish, Our Lady of Lourdes, in Palmira. At the beginning of May we began a discernment with five teenagers, 15-18 years. We had before us a number of ideas for different kinds of groups. One idea was presented each Saturday for a number of weeks and the young people had the week to discuss among themselves. One idea I presented was the Marist laity or Third Order of Mary.

When the day came for the young people to make their decision, they chose the Marist way and wanted to call it *Marist Youth Third Order.*

On Sunday June 4 we held our first meeting.

So now in Colombia the laity in the Marist family had come into being. What had attracted these young people? Various aspects, but underlying was the love and respect they had for Mary, mother of Jesus. The Colombians love Our Lady. They wanted to live the gospel with Mary at their side as a guide. They wanted to do their apostolate, study, work, without drawing attention, but still being able to enjoy themselves. It was, in other words, the Marist spirit which attracted them. I'm sure the Founder won't object but there was precious little said about him, just the presentation of his dream and no more. We are very careful on this point, because it is Mary's spirit, and not a cult built up around our Founder, that we offer to people. The following year, 1990, on the feast of Corpus Christi, each member gave his/her commitment at the parish Mass.

In 1991 our wonderful band of women, who had worked alongside us since our arrival in this area, were received into the Third Order. In all there are 30 members with six more who have begun to attend meetings and hopefully next year, 1993, will see them as Marists as well. Our chaplain is Fr. Bernardo Escobar.

All the members have an apostolate: teaching catechism, junior youth groups, studies, prayer groups and involvement in their parish. The parish priest remarked to me regarding the group in Palmira, "They are the yeast in the parish," and that is how we, the Marist Sisters, see our Marist laity — the yeast, the candle light wherever they are present.

For the very young children there is the *Semillas Maristas* (*Marist Seedlings*). This year a group for 14-15 year olds has begun. It has been named *Camino hacia María* (*Road to Mary*). Their aim: to live the gospel as Mary would, alongside of her, in their student lives. At Easter, if they wish to continue, they will make their commitment, and begin to put their formation into practice. They will each recruit five others, and from their group sow the seed of "Living as Mary would in today's world."

So over the eight years, our Marist family has creatively grown up alongside of us. Putting it in order it looks like this: *Semillas Maristas* (*Marist Seedlings*) — *Camino hacia María* (*Road to Mary*) — *Tercera Orden Juvenil Marista* (*Marist Youth Third Order*) — *Tercera Orden Laicos Maristas* (*Marist Laity Third Order*).

Before ending, I'm sure you have noticed that there has not been any special mention of men. (Apart from the *Juvenil Marista*). In July 1992 a young man, Alfredo, whose mother is a member, was received into the Marist family. His is a special story. Sister Marie-Yvonne had been visiting him for over a year, painfully, and gradually with joy, preparing him and his family for his final journey home. While sister was away, it was my privilege to take him communion. During one of these visits we talked about the Third Order. "I would like to belong, but I can't go to the meetings!" At my next visit, the family gathered around and Alfredo was received into the Third Order. The gospel chosen was the wedding feast of Cana. A few weeks later Alfredo died. The medal which he received never left him, and before closing the coffin, his mother and wife pinned it securely to his white shirt.

The Marist Family Ministry Team, in Australia, with Fr. Ron Nissen, S.M., as animator.

Origins — The Marist Family Ministry Team (MFMT) began in 1989-1990 with a group of 5 married couples and their families, a Marist Sister, plus several young singles, all committed to building up Christian family life and open to Mary's spirit in their lives and ministry. They are spread from Mackay (in Queensland) to Traralgon (in Victoria).

Activities — The MFMT comes together on three weekends a year (usually at Marist Centre, Toongabbie), variously for in-service in ministry skills development, retreat, review and planning. In between times, members collaborate to present the **Young Adults' Weekend**, the **Belonging Experience** (an adaptation of the Parish Renewal Weekend), and **"in home" programs** concerning family issues. A short monthly newsletter (edited by a Sydney couple), combined with a telephone "hotline" keeps members in good communication.

Vocations ministry — Since its inception, the Team has had a special interest in vocations promotion and support. Several couples have participated in the Costello/Birch workshops on **Vocations for Tomorrow's Church** and **Vocational Accompaniment**. One Queensland couple assists Fr. Ron Nissen, S.M., in the accompaniment of a prospective candidate in their area.

The Team conducts a monthly Taizé prayer vigil for vocations at Marist Centre. In May 1992, the MFMT in-service weekend was devoted to vocations ministry, involving reflection on the current vocations situation, Pope John Paul's latest letter, *Pastores Dabo Vobis*, and input on Marist vocations from Tony McCosker (the provincial). Each participant couple or single developed their own "mini pastoral plan" for vocations ministry.

Vision and spirituality — Animating the life of the MFMT is the conviction that Mary's spirit and way of doing things is for everyone. Team members are becoming increasingly familiar with Marist history, tradition, and spirituality. In 1991, several families and singles from the team formed a pilgrimage to the Marist places in France. At a weekend gathering shortly after the 1991 meeting with the Fathers' Council of the Society, the Team reflected on the major concerns of that Council (community life, partnership with laity, and vocations). There was an extraordinary resonance between the issues professed Marists face and those of the lay members of the MFMT.

Future — Each year, on or about the feast of Christ the King, the MFMT takes time off to review its life for the previous year, celebrate the fruits of ministry in that time and come up with a pastoral plan for the ensuing year of grace. Members renew their commitment for a further 12 months. It seems that the presence of Marist religious is a key value for these people. However, since co-responsibility holds a prominent place in the mentality of the MFMT, the future is very much in the hands of the team members themselves.

The ***Young Adults' Weekend*** *is described by a member of the Team, Miss Julie Jordan:*

As a Team we provide a weekend for young adults, those in their late teenage years and twenties. The weekend focuses on Christian values and on how they relate to strengthening our Catholic world.

First we invite everyone to spend quiet time and prayer time with our Lord, in the spirit of Taizé. Most of the weekend enables the people to experience quiet time, time out from home, work, and other distractions, to focus on certain topics; time to consider where their lives are presently, and how they can choose to be more involved as members in the Body of Christ.

Our recent Young Adults Weekend focused on:

1) *Lifestyle.* Discerning our own freedom and choices in the way we live daily, and how does the way we individually budget build up the Kingdom of God.

2) *Christian Sexuality.* Acceptance of our own sexuality, to be feminine or masculine, and our relationships with other people. To realise the importance and specialness our Church holds in her relationship with each vocation.

3) *Faith and Prayer.* What place does Mary have in our lives? What is our commitment to daily prayer? We, the Team, are able to share with young singles our growth and decisions in living our lives more fully as members of the Body of Christ. Also, the spirit of Mary is alive, as we lead our young adults on the "Rosary Walk." A time for each of us to be with each other and with our Lady as we say the rosary together, walking amidst nature, the trees, listening to the birds, etc. For each decade we dedicate a grace before our Lady, to ask for her help and guidance. Another precious moment is being part of and celebrating the intimacy of the Eucharist. These young adults come to acknowledge and focus more fully on sharing their responsibility as members of the Body of Christ and to grow spiritually in their faith.

What is happening in the Marist Sisters' sphere of influence in Australia, a report by Sister Mary Berise, S.M.

At the very heart of the whole endeavour is our Prayer Network — "Prayer Companions of the Marist Sisters," which now has 618 registered members. We keep in contact with them by two newsletters every year and a Christmas card. The newsletters contain news of the Sisters and their work, Marist spirituality and news of general Marist interest, including Marist laity. The first gathering of Prayer Companions took place at North Mackay on Our Lady's Assumption, 1992, and further gatherings are planned for the future on a regular yearly basis. Wherever there are clusters of Prayer Companions, we will open to them the possibility of forming some Marist laity groups.

The other "power house" of prayer besides our elderly Sisters at Marian House, is the large Marist laity group of elderly women and some men in the Gilroy Retirement Village, Merrylands, formed in 1982. They meet monthly for prayer and spiritual input by a variety of guest speakers mostly from the Marist religious family but also some diocesan and religious priests. They have an outreach of care and concern to the other people living around them. Wherever possible, they attend Marist gatherings, e.g., Fourvière celebrations.

Since 1980, the Sisters have conducted a ministry for the unborn with Prayer Cards for Expectant Parents and a specially worded one for single mothers and those in difficult situations. Now a card is in the planning for families where a child has died. Where possible a number of babies and other children are often dedicated to Mary in our chapels. This forms a link with young families.

The Marist Family Ministry involves lay people. In Merrylands West, a core group of married couples is meeting. In a kind of Marist Basic Christian Community, it combines Marist spirituality and family support, with parallel programmes for children and adults in a shared-meal atmosphere with some time for socializing, but also with an outreach to hurting and needy families. Another core group is composed of young couples in Melbourne, all Marist ex-students, a family group for young families from two or three parishes.

The Marian Mothers' Groups began in Merrylands West in 1983; other groups have been formed in Melbourne, Ferntree Gully, and in the Armadale/Malvern area. They have been using the Format and Tape/Leaflets of the New Zealand Marian Mothers' Groups and some local material based on Scripture and family values. In Gladstone, Queensland, there is a Filipino

Marian prayer group, which gives support to families of mixed Filipino/Australian marriages, along with home visitation. This group often uses the Word of Life Scripture commentary of "Mary's Work" (Focolare Movement) and other Marist material. Retreat days for mothers are held regularly also in Gladstone under the sponsorship of a unique team of Marist Fathers, Brothers and Sisters.

A Rosary group in Gladstone, which includes input on Marist spirituality and history, is going well. The Victorian core group of Marist Laity, which began in Bennettwood in 1989 with a New Zealand layman, Kevin Luxford, as the instigator, was unique as it comprised a core of all the Marist religious congregations with a larger group of lay people from all walks of life. They use the Frank McKay AMP model but have also, at their own request, had presentations of the Marist charism and history given by all of the Marist religious congregations and a special attempt at unraveling the history of the Marist lay branch. Every year, with the full cooperation of the parish priest, they organise and host the Fourvière celebrations for the wider Marist Family in the local parish church and hall.

Report by Fr. Ángel Antón Miravalles, S.M., on the Marist Missionary Community of Callao, Peru, January 1993.

The *Marist Missionary Community* began during the year 1989. Some youth in the parish groups of Santa Rosa, a Marist parish in Callao, used to meet one Sunday every month for reflection and prayer. Common topics were the laity, Marist spirituality, the missions, laity involved in the Marist mission. Some had the happy opportunity of participating in a national missionary congress for youth. Another had attended a lay national mission congress. During the year all participated in different experiences of mission in isolated and neglected parts of the country which had no pastoral agents for some years.

In the words of the group: "These experiences led us to feel that not only was it good to be committed lay persons, but we also needed to choose to be *missionaries* wherever we might be, especially among the poorest people, among those who are most alienated and neglected. We wanted to be missionaries with Mary, in Mary's way, integrated within the Marist family, united from the first with the Marist family as *lay people*. We understand that this has to be our contribution to the Church of today, to that Church of the last days which speaks to us of the ideal of the Marist project."

The lay people have adopted the name *Marist Missionary Community* because they want to be a *community* (to live as the first Christians, in love and understanding, so that the word of God would tell us what we need to do and that Eucharist would give us the strength to do it); *Marist* (to know Mary as a Mother and Model to be imitated in everything — in thinking, in speaking and doing; to live and announce the gospel in the style of Mary; to make a reality the utopia of the Marian People of Fr. Colin); and *missionary* (involved in the new evangelization, opting always for the marginalized and neglected; always ready to go on mission).

Today the *Marist Missionary Community* attempts to advance in accord with a *plan of life and mission*. It emphasizes attaining it in spite of mistakes, contradictions and setbacks, on the foundation of *prayer* (taste for God); *fraternity* (form a community for mission); *formation* (training for mission); *apostolate* (do the Work of Mary); and *poverty* (attentive to the cry of the poor).

Presently, the *Marist Missionary Community* expresses its evangelizing task in one of the marginal zones of the parish of Santa Rosa in Callao. During the year, especially in times of study and work vacations, it does missionary work in the Andes region where no priest can go.

Every three months the community holds a weekend retreat where themes of Marist spirituality are shared in prayer; there is evaluation with fraternal correction; the next three-months program is planned. The first Saturday of the month is dedicated to common prayer. The other weekly gatherings are concerned with pastoral matters and the other business of the community.

According to what they can do, the members take part in opportunities to deepen their faith and for pastoral formation. Some orient their professional studies to dedicating themselves full time to the mission as lay people.

The community is open to new members who, after a certain length of time, are invited to a gathering called *Nazareth*, where they can join the community. Some think of a firm commitment, with identification as a lay Marist and exclusive dedication to the mission to the marginalized and abandoned. On occasion some have entertained the possibility of living in common; but we need to give the Spirit time to decide.

The lay people are thankful for the welcome of the Marist Fathers and the Missionary Sisters of the Society of Mary. They have had some little contact with the Marist Brothers. The Marist Sisters are not in Peru. The consciousness of belonging to a common trunk and the same family is being reinforced. It costs a bit more to grow in awareness of our Marist identity as lay people.

Lay people request the religious to accompany them spiritually and to transmit to them the Marist spirituality and to support the signs of hope that arise. My presence has been as a spiritual adviser, accompanying them and collaborating with them.

Parish Pastoral Support Team, in Fiji, an island nation in the Pacific, is described by Fr. Michael Bransfield, S.M.

In Fiji we are developing an apostolate that serves the local Church and allows us to do it in the manner of Mary. We call it the *Parish Pastoral Support Team*. This initiative began very quietly in the parish of Lami, where there is a small Marist community: Paddy Bambrick is the parish priest, his brother Tom works for the matrimonial tribunal and helps with Masses and confessions, and Michael Bransfield and Kusitino Bobona are assistant priests.

Lami is not a "service-station" type parish. We see it as a platform for mission, finding ways of evangelising the marginalised while generously helping the priests, laity, and organisations of the archdiocese. The core team includes religious and laity. It is not a closed-off unit nor is it limited geographically or by Marist profession. Its members can live in different places, though a core secretariat group is needed to co-ordinate and distribute its services. It is very much a shared vision and community of effort. It is not a teaching unity apart from those who learn from it. Rather it works intimately with the parish, and its main contribution is "support," working like leaven from within.

It offers to help in any way a parish may wish, from comprehensive planning of a whole parish programme to piece-meal help for particular facets of parish life. The following are some of the areas for which it provides help: 1) The New Image of a parish programme proposed by the Movement for a Better World. 2) A spirituality based on our baptismal sharing in the passion and resurrection of Christ. 3) The unifying concept of Convergence Evangelism, mobilising the whole parish for evangelisation. 4) The Parish Cell system, providing a disciplined basic ecclesial community system directed towards evangelisation. 5) Various conversion experiences such as retreats, Parish Renewal, Choice, Antioch, Marriage Encounter, Retorno, Parish Empowerment weekend, etc. 6) Baptismal instruction programme. 7) Teaching, formation of formators, being resource persons, but opening all ministries to the laity. 8) Leadership training, formation in how to plan parish programmes.

The present stage of the Church's development in Oceania requires that we clearly accept that the local people are the owners of the local Church. They have full rights in policy and decision making. Our contribution is to ensure that "no one walks alone," that we actively support their initiatives and share our expertise. The core unity of the support team tries to model itself on Mary in thought, speech, and manner of acting. In the early Church, Mary was a presence of caring support, a listener and encourager, a questioner and source of reflection, a receiver of joys and disappointments. The ideal aimed at by the team is to enable all laity of a parish to do the work of Mary, in the manner of Mary. It is a ministry that is uniquely suited to our Marist spirituality and mission.

At the end of July 1989, Lami parish had a Parish Cell system of 28 cells, and the neighbouring parish of Lomary had 5 cells served from Lami. There is a plan to bring the Parish Cell system to Wairiki parish, for which the initial projection calls for 40 cells. The Pastoral Support Team is a response to the Church's call to every baptised person to be missionary.

Fr. Luís de la Cámara, the Provincial of the Marist Fathers in Spain, tells in January 1991 of the beginnings of lay Marist life there.

The method employed to begin some form of the Marist laity in Spain was a gathering of lay people with Marist priests. This was held in December 1990. The lay people came from where we (the Marist Fathers) have apostolic works. In all there were 64 lay people, 27 of whom were married and 14 were youths. Two days of meetings were held with four conferences, work in groups and celebrations of faith. The conferences were entitled: *Mary in the Church*, *Marists in the Church*, *Lay people in the Church*, and *Is a Marist laity possible?*

All who attended expressed interest in following the Marist way. One result of this gathering was that, in each place where there is a Marist community or where Marist Fathers are working, we are gathering groups of committed lay people who meet periodically to learn about Marist spirituality and to try to live, think, act, and feel as Mary. This is a process which takes time, and people move forward in different ways. There is an awareness that to follow Christ in the style of Mary, first it is really necessary to "follow Christ." We are finding it helpful to mark different stages of commitment with celebrations marked with signs or symbols which express the commitment, e.g. Bible, light, formula of commitment.

A concern is to avoid the participants seeing themselves as belonging to "elite groups." We wish to see them integrated into the parochial and collegial community. We also want to avoid any form of "favoritism." Mary, creator of unity!

In these efforts we use some material put together in Spanish by Fr. Ángel Antón called "Marist laity: to do the work of Mary."

Fraternités Maristes *in Burundi. Information from Fr. Alain Forissier, S.M.*

The Marist Fraternities in Burundi — and at Kiliba, Zaire — are Fraternities of secondary-school (lycée) youth. They meet together twice per month under the direction of an animator who is chosen by the young people themselves on an annual basis. These young people are often involved in parish movements, absorbed by their studies in an environment where traveling is done on foot most of the time and often in the rain. These factors must be taken into account with regard to the meetings, which are limited in time and follow an identical rhythm. The plan of the meetings is: prayer, exchange on the way the charter has been lived, teaching (e.g. on praying the psalms or the texts of the gospels concerning Mary), information about the fraternities.

By way of illustration, the Fraternity of the Lycée de Rohero has taken as the central point of its annual charter: "How to live hidden and unknown?" The young people explained their manner of doing this:

▪ At home, an employee does all the work. However, one day he was away on an errand. I washed the dishes in his place, without saying anything.

▪ I am in the choir. One morning during the week we were singing at a funeral Mass. It was explained to us that there was to be another one that evening, and we were asked if we could return. The choir refused. Then I said to myself: "Marists should do what others do not wish to do." And I came back to sing at the Mass.

▪ While passing near the Church, I saw that very few of the team of women responsible for cleaning it were there. I entered then, and, saying nothing, I took a broom. When the work was almost finished, I left quickly to avoid being questioned about it.

The Marist Volunteer Program operates in the United States of America

The name Marist Volunteer Program speaks about the nature and purpose of this program.

1. Marist. The founders of the Marists, each in their own way, felt that God wanted to do something through them in the manner and under the name of Mary. Those first Marists conceived of the Marist project as the work of Mary and used the image of a tree with many branches to speak about the diversity of its parts. Part and parcel of this original understanding was the role of lay people who would share in a concrete manner in the work and spirit of the Marist project.

2. This present program is a joint effort of the different branches of the Marist family. In its own modest way, this program attempts to do what the first Marists saw as part of their mission: a unified effort of the different Marist branches working together to extend the mercy of God to others through an experience of Marist life. In our day, the unified efforts of Marists working together draws attention to the solidarity of mission which is present among all the branches of our Marist family. United with Mary, we extend compassion and mercy to all, especially the most neglected and abandoned, until the Kingdom of her Son is fulfilled. Because of the urgency of this task in our day, we as Marists invite others to work alongside and in communion with the mission we have been given.

3. The men and women who accept the invitation to become Marist volunteers, come as Christians who wish to strengthen and enrich their baptismal call as members of the Church. We

invite them to share in an experience of community by praying, living and working with us, and in doing so we open ourselves to developing a broader vision of community and to fulfill the prophetic call the Church has recognized in our charism.

4. Experiencing the prayer, the life and the familial sharing of the Marist tradition hopefully will encourage the volunteers to bring Mary's spirit to the world today. Our sincerest hope and prayer is for the communication and acceptance of the Marist charism in one way or another among the volunteers through the people they serve. It is our hope that many of the volunteers will continue some form of association with the Marist movement throughout their life.

The director of the Volunteer program, Br. Frank Kelly, F.M.S., reports that there were about 75 requests for information about the program. Ten volunteers have been accepted into the program for the year 1993, seven men and three women. They will be involved in teaching, campus ministry and child care. Health insurance, room and board are provided, and stipends are worked out individually.

Course on Marist Spirituality in Ireland

Marists in Ireland provided a course in Marist spirituality for laity in 1992-1993. The purpose of the course was *to offer an opportunity to people to discover and deepen, in a warm environment, what in them is leading them towards a Marist spirituality.* The discovery was for those who are beginning. The deepening was for those who have some familiarity with the spirituality. (*See above, pp. 65-83, for the themes studied in this course.*)

Each session focused on one of the Marist symbols — those phrases or images that Marists repeat to each other (for instance: hidden and unknown, gracious choice, Mary in the newborn Church, tree with many branches, instruments of mercy, etc.). It was a good method for releasing the spirituality and giving people the same "coat hangers" we use ourselves. It was then up to the people themselves to translate the spirituality into their own daily lives. All we provided was the formation.

The course was run in two different locations, by two different groups. It took place one evening per month, and each session lasted about 90 minutes. The two groups took different approaches. Each planning group included Marist clergy and Marist laity (two people in one location, four in the other). The planning group met in between each session. At each session a document was given to the participants, which tried to take on board the questions raised in peoples' minds. This document was prepared between sessions.

One group invited a different guest speaker for each session, a Marist who had a grasp of the particular symbol under discussion. They began with prayer and a scriptural reflection on Mary. After input from the guest speaker, they broke into small groups for a short time. Then there was a general discussion with the whole group. Finally there was a short review of the previous session, in order to help the planning group.

In the second location, the format of each session differed, according to the topic under discussion. This group explored the symbol under discussion with a presentation by the organizing committee. Discussion in a large group followed, sometimes in smaller groups first. Once again, prayer formed an important part of the proceedings, but this time they ended with prayer, mostly silent prayer, with Scripture reading and a hymn. Depending on the session, the time allotted to discussion and prayer varied. Sometimes the prayer was longer; sometimes, the discussion.

The course did not try to establish new Marist groups, or form people into one large group. It was left up to the participants themselves to make of it what they will. It was an exercise in the formation of laity, and was respectful of their freedom. The course sought to knit together the experience of being a lay person in the Church today, with the deposit of Marist spirituality we have been given. "Creative fidelity" might be a good summary of what was attempted. We tried to be faithful to the Marist charism, yet left the creativity, or lay embodiment of the charism, up to lay people themselves. Any additional help was given outside the course, through the provincial animators (of whom there are two) and lay collaborators. This included providing retreat days on Marist themes.

Familia Marista (Marist Family) is a new development of Marist laity in Mexico.

Fr. Pedro Herrasti, S.M., reports on recent developments of Marist laity in Mexico and their plans for the future.

When, at the *Centro Politécnico de Proyección* (the Marist campus ministry center at the Polytechnical University), some students asked us about the Society of Mary, we decided to present it to all of the Center's Apostolic Groups [*Grupos Apostólicos*] in a two-day retreat. Among those who worked on the project were Edgar Anguiano and Pedro Alarcón, then seminarians but now ordained priests.

Once all the Apostolic Groups had made the Marist retreat, there arose quite naturally the idea of founding the Marist Family [*Familia Marista*] about which Guillermo Múñoz has written (*see pp. 16-20*).

It needed to be given a new identity, but this was no easy task. Together, we sought carefully and finally drew up a few statutes and an annual promise for adhering to the Society of Mary (see below).

Besides the Marist Family at the *Centro Politécnico*, composed mainly of young people, we have two other communities of older Marist tertiaries who follow the rules of Fr. Eymard and are directed by Fr. Cruz Bailón, one at the parish of the Immaculate Conception in Clavería and the other in Toluquilla, in the state of Jalisco; both are marvels for having survived the vagaries of time. While we respect the "Third Order" style of these communities composed entirely of women, we also see the need to move the Marist laity forward in a new way.

We shall continue with the retreats which we can call "initiation retreats" to which lay people from all our ministries are invited. For the lay people who are already Marists, we shall give "retreats for deepening" on various themes, such as the history of our Society, Mariology, Colinian spirituality, etc.

The following are the Statutes of Mexico's Familia Marista:

1. The lay Marist adopts as his own the spirituality expressed in numbers 49 and 50 of the Constitutions of the Society of Mary.

2. So as to live out the Marist spirituality, the lay member attends the monthly meeting of the Marist Family.

3. Every day, he will spend a few minutes at spiritual reading about Mary or meditating on the Bible or some book about Mary.

4. Daily, the Marist will pray the Angelus and the Rosary or part of it.

5. As often as possible, he will take part in the Eucharist and receive Holy Communion, especially at Sunday Mass.

6. He will participate in the works of the Marist Family Apostolate.

7. Every month, he will try to receive the Sacrament of Reconciliation and spiritual direction from some Marist priest.

8. Every year, on September 12, the Feast of the Holy Name of Mary, he will renew for a year his promise of belonging to the Society of Mary. This may be done in a special community ceremony or privately, and he will inform the director of the Marist Family.

Promise made by members of the Familia Marista:

"I, ______, before you, reverend Father and the Marist Family, promise to God our Lord, for one year, to live in the grace of God, in the style of Mary, Mother of God and our Mother; to work ardently at evangelization, according to the spirituality proper to the Society of Mary.

"My God, help me to carry out what I propose to do. Mary, my Mother, I am yours, intercede for me with your Son and my Savior, Jesus Christ. Amen."

A method developed by Fr. Roland Lajoie, S.M., Marist laity director of the Boston Province of Marist Fathers, United States of America.

My first challenge in developing Colinian ideas of Marist laity was to ask myself, "To whom shall I go to share this message and mission of Marist laity?" Through being spiritual director on a Cursillo weekend, I was called to several parishes through the laity who participated in the weekend. Because they heard of the message of mercy and hope through our Marist Story, they went to their pastors and asked them to invite me to their parishes to bring the message of mercy and to do good "in a hidden and unknown way."

To introduce pastors and faithful to the Marist spirit for lay people, I was brought in to give parish missions and retreats, a necessary period of time to convey the vision and the mission through a process.

The method that I have found that has worked is to give a parish retreat using the mysteries of the rosary, as a way to develop Marist spirituality, using the instrument that lay people can easily relate to in a practical and reflective way. The mysteries of the rosary help me to introduce the parishioners to the spirituality of Mary from Nazareth to Pentecost.

At Saturday and Sunday Masses, they are introduced to the spirituality of the Society of Mary, and the laity are invited to adopt it for their daily lives and their call to mission.

Monday of the week we develop the joyful mysteries: a message of joy and hope to be called, as Mary was called at the Annunciation. Mary's call to openness to the spirit.

Tuesday: the sorrowful mysteries: self-confrontation and hope through mercy and compassion. "Follow him; do whatever he tells you."

Wednesday: the glorious mysteries: Go forth to love and serve the Lord by your presence and grace in a hidden and unknown way — Contemplating Mary in the mysteries of Nazareth and Pentecost and her role at the end of time. The lay people come to share her zeal for her Son's mission in his struggle against evil, and to respond with promptness to the most urgent needs of God's people. (S.M. Constitutions, no. 8).

Throughout the week there is adoration of the Blessed Sacrament, ongoing availability for the sacrament of reconciliation and a closing Mass and consecration by the pastor of the parish, who is invited to further the vision and mission presented to his parish during the week. There is an initial introduction to the Marist laity for a parish during the week. Parishioners desiring to have a more personal experience of the Marist spirituality for the laity are asked to give their names for a more focused Marist seminar presented at a later date.

The pastors of the parishes are encouraged to continue leading their flocks in the spirit of the Marist mission. A healing Mass and a consecration of the parish to the Blessed Mother closes the Marist mission experience.

Many pastors, pleased with the spirituality presented, invite me for a second mission where the Marist spirituality is presented in the style of a Life in the Spirit Seminar.

Marie-Jeunesse: a way of living. In Québec, Canada, Fr. Jean Claude Trottier, S.M., has been involved in this.

In December 1982 on the occasion of the birthday of one of them, about a dozen young people from Québec decided to get together to celebrate the occasion. The "Réal gang," which one day would be called *Marie-Jeunesse* (Mary-Youth), was born. Réal Lavoie was a man of simple but strong faith, and was living with some Marist Fathers and had read some of what Fr. Jean-Claude Colin had to say. This led to other things!

What was this Marie-Jeunesse about? Very simply it was about a group of young people searching for an ideal, a group for whom Jesus Christ had become the center of their lives and who wanted to tell others, especially young people, about Jesus, by living like Mary. Their mission: among young people, to continue the work of Mary; to be her heart, her hands, her smile, her welcome, her tenderness. In a word, to enable other children of God to come alive. Concretely this translated itself into a daily explosion of celebrations, of sporting and cultural activities, all seasoned with the salt of the gospel and the richness of prayer and the Eucharist.

In 1986 a first house of welcome for youth was opened in a working-class area of Québec. In 1988 it gave out over 10,000 meals to young people in search of food, friendship, and a meaning to life. The group began to grow over the province of Québec, and numbered 200 consecrated members (1989), of whom many have responded to a special call from the Lord to enter the seminary or religious novitiates.

During the years Marie-Jeunesse has expanded to include adults, children, elderly people, priests, and university people, all of whom consecrate their lives to God in whatever position they may be, to become the family of Mary, so that now they have Mary-Elderly, Mary-Families, Mary-University. Marie-Jeunesse is the parable of the mustard seed, Québec version.

Fr. Thomas Muni is the parish priest of Sigave. Fr. François Jaupitre is parish priest of Alo. Both are in Futuna, an island in the Pacific. They report on the Third Order in Wallis and Futuna. Futuna was first evangelized by the Marist Fathers, and is where St. Peter Chanel, S.M., was martyred in 1841.

Tiesolo (Futuna) and Tiasolo (Wallis) is how the Third Order is called here. The members, men and women, are very numerous and the Third Order is by far the biggest Church group in the diocese (between 800 and 1000 members). It is present in each of the five parishes. It has been implanted for a long time and is still very alive.

Here the Third Order is the traditional type. There is a monthly recollection; assistance at Mass for the Marian feasts, the feasts of the apostles and the first Saturday of each month;

an annual retreat of 3 days; daily recitation of the rosary; regular meetings. Beyond these exercises there is an emphasis on making an effort to develop a Christian family life with the education and religious instruction of the children. Members are requested to give good example in their villages especially with regard to conjugal fidelity and in the struggle against alcohol abuse.

The Third Order plays a prominent role in the life of parishes and of the diocese. A great many members are active in parish life, in the liturgy, and in works of charity. They are a valuable support to the priests. Most of the country's priestly and religious vocations have come from Third-Order families.

It is the parish priest who is the chaplain and animator of the Third Order in the parish. Of the five parish priests, two are Marists and three are diocesan priests. A Marist Father is diocesan director.

There is a council of the Third Order in each parish consisting of two presidents (man and woman), two secretaries, two treasurers, novice-master, novice-mistress. The rest of the council is made up of two representatives from each village. This council is more or less important according to the size of the parish. The council concerns itself with projects of the broader community, the parish, or the Marist group itself.

The Third Order here is very highly organized and structured. It is restricted to adults. There is the period of training and probation under the novice-master or novice-mistress. After the Council judges the person fit for membership, he/she makes a profession or commitment. The demands made are high in the call to perfection; and, if someone is obviously not taking this seriously, he/she may be asked to quit for a time or even indefinitely.

Fr. Peter Allen, S.M., describes a group in England

The Marist Fathers have had the direction of the Catholic National Shrine of Our Lady in England since 1968. The Anglicans, too, have their own Shrine in the same place, the village of Walsingham, in the East coast. Devotion to Our Lady of Walsingham has grown rapidly in recent years and thousands of pilgrims flock here every year. Some of the local people of the village, who belong to different Christian Churches, found that pilgrims often share their problems and burdens. This moved them to want to understand more about the Shrine and its spirituality, and so seek help to be able to do more for these pilgrims. This resulted in a group being formed by Fr. Peter Allen in 1986. About 15 people have met each week since then to meditate on the scriptures, to pray for the needs of pilgrims, and to give each other support in their Christian living. This group is open to all and is ecumenical. A diocesan priest, Fr. Digby Samuels (Westminster diocese) spent about two years in Walsingham as a member of the group.

The spirituality that animates them is that of Mary, particularly at the Annunciation, as she waited in faith on the Lord, pondering his Word and bringing Him to birth in her life. They see their role to be like that of Mary in the midst of the people, being their support in faith and prayerful intercession. Drinking in the Marist spirit together, these village people find they are able to deepen their own life of union with God and also have a sense that they are doing the work of Mary in helping the troubled pilgrims who visit the Shrine. The bishop, the Rt. Rev. Alan Clark, has been very encouraging to the group and has given them the use of a house which serves as a "poustinia," a special place of prayer.

Marian Mothers Groups in New Zealand are animated by Fr. John Allardyce, S.M.

It is clear that the family, "the domestic church" has needs which are more urgent than in former times. Family life is under pressures unknown to earlier generations. Women see their role, as wives and mothers, devalued by a society which once supported them. Many women are made to feel ill at ease with their role as mothers and they find domestic work held in less esteem than in earlier times. If the "great bearers of the values of society" (Paul VI) lose confidence in their vocation, the results are serious for both Church and society.

Fr. Allardyce began groups for mothers in 1981. Beginnings were slow and there were mistakes and misunderstandings. Groups began to proliferate in 1983. They are scattered about city parishes and country districts and some groups also exist in Australia. There are now more than 80 of them and the numbers involved are in excess of a thousand. The growth and persistence of these groups is probably largely due to the fact that they meet a great need in peoples' lives. These Marian groups for mothers help to provide an experience of Christian community for mothers. This must have some religious focus in keeping with their vocation as wives and mothers. The experience of sharing faith and prayer leads to mutual support, witness, encouragement; it offers opportunity for catechesis and helps to build up the faith of the domestic and local churches.

They are parish-based and vary in membership from about 6 to 20 members. They are not focused in any way on being explicitly Marist. None of the mothers would consider themselves Marists in any sense. The general title given to the movement is *Marian Mothers*, but there is a wide variety in the names used by individual groups. Here is an extract from the newsletter of 1992:

> Let's remember that the Marist groups do not belong to the Society of Mary (priests and brothers) as such, but rather are part of the parish communities. They do not exist solely for the spiritual advancement of their members but have an active mission which makes them Marian and authentic. In our case, we have a mission of mercy/compassion and we must also promote unity and "solidarity" in the parish community of which we are part.

The groups work very simply, but they have a definite organization. They are led by a "convener" who has contact with the Marist Centre, from which Fr. John and Sr. Catharina work. A cassette-tape, leaflet and a newsletter are sent monthly to all groups. Some groups meet from 10 a.m. till midday; others, in the evenings. Discussion points relate directly to the taped material. (In November 1992 a tape on forgiveness was made by a local group for the use of the others). The tapes and leaflets try to provide something that appeals to them as wives (many are solos) and mothers. The idea is that they minister to each other and build up their faith and come to support the local churches. Something about Mary is given slowly, emphasizing her attitudes. The groups have spread mainly by word of mouth and family transfers. (Canada has a group going because of a woman who was in a local group before transferring there).

Fr. Allardyce visits these groups from time to time, for animation and encouragement. They operate with the approval and encouragement of the bishops and in unity with the parish priests (*see pp. 51-52; also, pp. 26-27*). These are the topics on the tapes for 1992:

How are you singing your song?
Mary — What does she mean to you?
Jesus Christ loves you
Your man and religion
Where are you, God?
Open home foundation
Let's celebrate motherhood
Forgiveness

There are a number of Marist lay groups in France. They have lay leadership. Fr. Jacques Arfeuillère is the delegate of the Marist Fathers to the lay Marist movements.

During the years 1960-1965, the traditional Third Order experienced a very important change, notably under the influence of Father Touzet and some lay people of Paris around the area of the Chapel of Notre-Dame des Anges. These groups took a name more adapted to the modern mentality: *Fraternités Maristes*, and had a bulletin whose title was *Lettre aux Fraternités Maristes* [*Letter to the Marist Fraternities*]. Every month the bulletin had a theme for meditation, reflections on the Marist spirit, items of news, etc.

A little later, in 1977, the *Fraternités Maristes* created their own association thus growing in autonomy. The laity, while remaining close to the Marist Fathers, created an organization for themselves, with those in leadership chosen from among themselves during a Congress held every three years.

The *Fraternités Maristes* were composed at this stage of people of every age (men, women, celibates and couples). Many of the members were young. There must have been up to a thousand members in France. However, nowadays the *Fraternités Maristes* comprise about 300 members in France and Belgium who remain very attracted to Marist spirituality, but most of the members are getting old.

A little after 1980, the review (*Lettre aux Fraternités Maristes*) was opened up to other groups close to the Marists. It became the bulletin *Échanges Maristes* [*Marist Exchanges*], which is noted for the quality of its contents. It is a monthly with a circulation of about 500.

It was at this time that other groups of lay Marists came into being:

▪ the *communautés élargies* ['enlarged communities']: entire Marist communities of Marist Fathers opened their doors to lay people for a common reflection, prayer, friendship. Only the groups in Toulon have continued in this link with the Marists, although individual members of other groups still have contact.

▪ *lay associates*: some lay people requested to be *associates* of the Society of Mary: this was a situation recognized by the Provincial Chapters of 1981 and 1985, binding the associates to the Society by participating in its mission, with the associates making a financial contribution to the expenses of the Province.

▪ the *Confrérie Sainte Marie* is a group of about thirty lay people which was begun at the Marist school (Externat Sainte Marie) in Lyons. Mostly teachers or other educators in the school, they want to draw inspiration from the Marist spirit in their work of education.

- *l'Union Mariste séculière*: a small group of consecrated people (about ten), founded by Father Prués in Lyons.

In 1988 it seemed a good idea to try to coordinate these groups a little. On the occasion of a gathering at La Neylière at Pentecost, a coordinating group was organized; and by spring 1992 an association of Marist lay people was set up — not to fuse the groups but to lead them to recognize one another and to meet. This has caused tensions but, after explanations were made, has shown positive promise. It was this coordinating group which proposed a two-day encounter in 1991 on the Marist theme of mercy. The 56 participants (of whom 40 were lay people) were there to share reflections and experiences on the theme. At the Assembly of the Province of the Marist Fathers in August 1992, there were fifteen lay persons present. It was decided to continue working on the "partnership" of lay and religious Marists. The Marist lay association sponsored another meeting on October 30-31, 1993, with reflection focused on the theme "The Magnificat today."

An initiative of promise in the Netherlands. (1993)

There has been something stirring the lives of four young Dutch people in the past few years. At the origin of this were weekly prayer meetings of a group of students of the school, *Marianum*, held every Saturday night in the chapel of the school. Some alumni of this group, scattered in different places because of their studies, kept in contact with one another. They had the desire to meet again to read some scripture together and to share on spiritual themes. From this, about three years ago, a group called *De Westerhelling* was born. Two members of this group, Conny van Zanten and Marion Korenromp, requested Father Fons de Block, S.M., to guide them in the spiritual attitude of the Marists. This coincided with the appearance of the book *Maristen* (1990). This book gave a historical outline of the Marist Fathers and the Marist Brothers, with emphasis on specific aspects. Meanwhile Hanneke Honselaar and André Stuart joined the group with the goal of penetrating together the characteristics of being a Marist.

A weekend of reflection was held at the convent of the Poor Clares at Megen. The results of the sharings were put together in a small document which offers the reflections of these young people on Fourvière, Cerdon and Le Bugey and what these Marist moments and also the person of Mary mean in their lives.

This document was discussed by the working group of the Marist Fathers/Marist Brothers. The members of this group and others who have read it have reacted positively.

These young people have received official recognition as Marists by the Marist Fathers and Marist Brothers in the Netherlands. On April 13, 1993, this Marist group had its official recognition ceremony which was an occasion of great celebration for the Marists in the Netherlands. Three lay Marists from Cologne, Germany, also joined in the festivities.

Fr. Dennis J. Steik is Co-director of the Marist Laity/Third Order, San Francisco Province of the Marist Fathers in the United States of America.

In 1988 Fr. Steik was director of the Newman Center in Azusa, California, which is a Campus Ministry center. He was not sure how to go about it but someone told him that Fr. Colin was a man of *praxis*, a man who learned by doing — just begin, reflect on your experience, trust the process and people who come together; folks will give shape to the group in a way that addresses their interests and needs.

This is a brief adapted summary of the model that evolved:

Session 1. Personal introduction and sharing of expectations. From their experience of Marists, participants express what they see as Marist characteristics in a word or short phrase. The Marist story is told.

Session 2. Each person tries to get in touch with his/her personal experience and answers for her/himself in one sentence the following questions: When have you experienced being ministered to and what was it like? When have you experienced the Church being genuinely Church? When have you experienced God in your life and what was it like? Each person's three sentences are placed on newsprint around the room, and each person reads his/hers in turn. Then the group can share reflections on what has been heard. What are the similarities? Unique aspects? What was learned?

Session 3. Everyone is handed out a typed-up copy of all the sentences from the last session and these are read in silence. Then connections of the themes around ministry, Church, and spirituality are made to the Marist story, Marist approach to ministry, Marist way of being Church, of growing spiritually.

Session 4. A copy of some material about lay ministry is handed out and, after time has been given for reading and digesting, it is discussed. Particular focus can be put on the question: "How does this relate to the themes of the Marist spirit, the whole world Marist, Colin's vision of building 'a new Church'?"

Sessions 5 and 6. Use round table prayer, and play a tape on ministry, evangelization. Relate to Marist material and draw out the implications for Church and ministry.

Sessions 7 and 8. Presentation of "Mariology in today's Church," followed by discussion.

Session 9. Telling our stories — giving flesh to the work in the marketplace. Simply have individuals describe their own busy schedules of work and daily demands. See how Maristness fits in. Sharing on how the spirit of Mary colors and even transforms daily responsibilities.

Session 10. Presentation of Colinian vision for Marist laity. Discussion on this.

Session 11. Take a conversion story, and see Marist qualities and values in it. How can I apply to my own values, family, work, ministry. Discussion.

Session 12. Where do we go from here? What process for meeting in the future? Possible resources: *The Age of Mary* by Jan Snijders, S.M., *Marist Laity* by Frank McKay, S.M.

(Some of the participants at session 10 spoke of their desire for some public commitment ceremony or ritual, preferably at Eucharist. There was also an expressed desire on the part of some for a visible sign or symbol that could be worn identifying them as members of the Marist family.)

Another group, centered in Glendora, California, grew out of a number of college students from the Newman Center in nearby Azusa..

Fr. Michael Galinada, S.M., was appointed to work in campus ministry at the Newman Center. He attended a course in Marist spirituality given at Framingham, Massachusetts. Enthused by the vision of Fr. Colin for lay people, he began to share this with some of the college students. They in turn were enthused and began to absorb this spirit of Mary and began to consider themselves Marists. When the Marist Fathers had to move out of the Newman Center, the students did not wish to let this die among them, so they managed to get the use of a room at St. Lucy's Priory in nearby Glendora for meetings. They call themselves *Our Lady of Mercy, a Community of Marist Laity.* They continue inviting college students (through notices sent by mail and other means) for evenings of reflection on the Scriptures, for shared prayer and social gatherings (featuring presentations and discussions on current social problems), and for a monthly Marist Vision gathering. They consider themselves a Marian corps of Mercy and are eager to share their Marist spirituality with other people of their age.

***Friends of the Marists organized to perform a social work in the Cooperative* Il Ricino *— in Moncalieri, Italy — a report by Fr. Antonio Ayrò, S.M., and members of* Il Ricino.**

"Our cooperative chose a name which for us is highly symbolic: the castor-oil plant (*il ricino*) is the small plant that God made sprout over the head of Jonah to provide shade in the middle of the desert. When Jonah chose to make it a refuge under which to stretch out rather than a mere refreshment along the way, God caused the castor-oil plant to dry up.

"The risk we run when we are comfortable in a community is to relax in a situation of dependency and passive care.

"For us community is a place of passage in which are offered the instruments to change, to shore up resources, to establish relations with persons and with the environment, and when these objectives seem to have been reached, the **castor-oil tree** should die for those who have benefited from it.

"Within this framework, the community welcomes pregnant women and women with babies, offering them a favorable climate in which to live out their maternity, framing with them a family environment which might restore security and the independence to take up again their own way of life."

This is the *magna carta* of a group of friends of the Marists, who, accepting the invitation and proposal of the Marist community of Villa Santa Maria of Moncalieri, took up the challenge of setting up a work of hospitality and accompaniment to young women in difficulty, a work which has been in operation since October 1991.

The Fathers of Villa Santa Maria thought up the project and made available to the group a house formerly used to house the Marist Sisters. From the very beginning the Fathers conceived the project as radically autonomous from the Marist community and proposed to their friends that they assume complete responsibility and direction.

To this end, a written contract was prepared to define reciprocal competencies and responsibilities: there is even a standard contract between the Fathers and the legally constituted cooperative covering the lease of the house.

The Marist community at Moncalieri assumes a support and accompaniment role relative to the group and also supplies spiritual care. Presently, the group meets periodically (every 15 days) to journey together in the faith; other moments of meeting are celebrations (Christmas, Easter, celebration of the sacraments, Marist feast days, etc.) and are open to other persons interested in the work and desirous of collaborating.

The cooperative is composed of 13 members and avails itself of the collaboration of 5 educators (among whom is a Marist Sister) and of an ample group of volunteers.

Besides conducting the social project itself the group is strongly involved in promoting and forming the volunteers, and have organized training courses and moments when people can gather to have a first look. Every Sunday afternoon one person from the cooperative and the Sister are present to receive persons who come to visit, know the community and offer their help.

The group also organizes cultural events — concerts and theatrical productions — to advertise the work and raise money to finance concrete initiatives aimed at consolidating and improving the social project.

The number of women guests is 8 plus their babies or baby to be born. The spirit of the family of Nazareth and the manner in which Mary welcomed the Word are the models which inspire the style of welcome and support-accompaniment given to these young women.

Fr. Bernd Kordes, S.M., has been involved in the form of Marist laity called* Marianisches Apostolat *(Marian Apostolate) in Germany for many years.

There are about 400 members of the *Marianisches Apostolat*. They pray together and share their faith and prayer experience when they meet once a month, once a week, or even more frequently. One section is made up of people living alone, spread all over Germany; some of them come together regularly for seminars or spiritual exercises, once in springtime, once in autumn, both in the north and in the south.

The majority of members are women, many of them older women; but more recently one group has successfully involved husbands. New groups also have young people.

Each group has its own character and is independent. Some are very alive and seek new members: every year they have additional numbers. Some members, who are far from groups, live the Marist life very intensely.

Two groups are in the happy position that the parish priest encourages and supports them, and is himself a member of the Marianisches Apostolat. One of them was made an honorary member; and, gladly accepting this, got his mother to join.

Groups appear to bond together better when they have a communal apostolate, and they can exchange their experiences and support one another in prayer. Many pray together once a week or more often or hold scripture sessions, or share their experiences of faith and daily life.

Also among the isolated members, we can distinguish those who are very conscious of the group and are in telephone or letter contact with them; others are silently faithful and only give an occasional indication of how much they appreciate the contact with the group.

My contact with these groups and individuals is primarily through the quarterly publication *Marianisches Apostolat*, which encourages exchange between members; i.e. members are invited to contribute something in writing, linking their life and faith witness to the theme of the next issue of the publication. There are also news items, reflections, material on Marist spirituality by Andrea Pichlmeier (a lay Marist, *see pp. 14-15, above*), and a lead article written by the Animator of the Marist Laity for Germany. The publication is sent to about 500 addresses and is well received.

Marist Spirituality Groups, Third Order of Mary, Italy.

In Italy, the directors of the Third Order of Mary have blended the insights of Fr. Colin with existing structures to form the *Gruppi di Spiritualità Marista* — Marist Spirituality Groups. Fr. Franco Messori, on the basis of a longer work by Fr.

Bartolomeo Bardessono, has written "To Live Her Life," from which we take the following extracts:

The second Vatican Council has committed the entire Church to put on a more Marian face in its internal and external behavior: advocating not triumphalism but simplicity, brotherhood and the spirit of service. In this way the Council was in harmony with the intuitions of Fr. Colin, who had dared to say: "The Society [of Mary] must begin a new Church over again."

The Marist movement, despite its small numbers and simplicity of means, feels called to become the animator of this "new Church," from the inside, as it were, as Mary was the animator of the primitive community. The Marist apostle not only desires to co-operate with all other Catholic forces but also to communicate to them his own spirit, the spirit of Mary, convinced that it constitutes a richness for the whole Church and that its spread complies with a concrete desire of Mary for today's Christianity, viewed in the light of the Christianity of the last days.

The members of the Third Order have an important role to play in this because they are able to come into contact with people of every class and belong to every type of organization.

Rule of Life. The spirit is the key! The Third Order of Mary wants to bring its members to Christian perfection and to guide them to the apostolate according to the model of the life led by Mary at Nazareth and among the Apostles.

It will offer its full support to the local Church to which it belongs, to the local pastor and to whatever apostolic and charitable initiatives in which it can become engaged. It will do everything in its power to ensure that the whole Fraternity acts as an integrating and constructive element of the Christian and human community to which it belongs.

At the same time, it will not fail to become involved in the life and works of the Society of Mary in Italy and in the world, realizing that it is a member and participant with full rights and responsibilities.

To live as Mary and according to her spirit, however, is a task which demands commitment and constancy. To sustain oneself in this ideal, the tertiary will strive to remain faithful to certain practices recommended by the T.O.M.:

1. Greeting Mary morning and evening by reciting three *Hail Marys*. It is advisable to add one of the more beautiful Marian prayers, *We fly to your protection* or the *Hail Holy Queen*.

2. Dedicating at least a quarter of an hour each day to meditation.

3. The daily recitation of the Rosary (5 mysteries) is highly recommended, though not obligatory.

4. Examination of conscience at the moment of evening prayer or at another time during the day.

5. Participation in the monthly retreat of the Fraternity led by the Father Director.

6. Taking part in the Feast of the Holy Name of Mary, which is the patronal feast of the Society of Mary, solemnly celebrated in all Marist houses on September 12.

7. Requesting the celebration, where and by whom one wishes, of an annual Mass for the deceased of the T.O.M. Moreover, participating in the Mass for the deceased of one's own Fraternity, which the President will take care to request during the first days of November. The Fraternity will have a Mass offered for all deceased members, a Mass which the members will strive to attend.

Various Categories. One can belong to the T.O.M. in various ways: (1) as *associated individuals*; (2) as fraternities properly so-called or *Marist Spirituality Groups*; (3) as *Nazareth Families* (families whose members are consecrated to Mary by an official act and as a group, and who commit themselves to live the life led by Mary at Nazareth and among the Apostles, with some exterior practices in common to remind them of their consecration); (4) as *Affiliated Groups* (specialized movements of youth, men, women, seminarians or priests, who, though they pursue their own purpose with their own organization and style, nevertheless strive to practice the spirit of Mary, accepting some points of the T.O.M. rule as a way of manifesting their affiliation); (5) as *Conjoined Persons* (persons inscribed in the "register of intentions recommended" to the prayers of the Fraternity, for example, expectant mothers, for a happy birth; babies about to be born, for the grace of Baptism; sinners, for their conversion; and persons in grave difficulty, especially of a spiritual or moral kind.

Apostolate. The primary end of the Third Order of Mary is the personal sanctity of its members to be realized in the world in accord with Marist ideals, that is, in the spirit of Mary.

Since charity and zeal are the fundamental virtues of every Christian, the tertiary will necessarily feel drawn to the apostolate in the example of her whom Marist tradition always recognized as "the support of the Church" from its beginning until the end of time.

The Third Order of Mary does not propose to its members any specific apostolate of its own. Rather, it invites them, in accord with the exhortation of the Church, to present themselves as volunteers at the disposition of their own dioceses and parishes, rendering useful service to their apostolates in the best way possible. Inspired by Father Colin's ideal, they will be happy if the fact that they belong to the Marist Third Order remains unknown to those with whom they collaborate, even if in fact this is the very leaven which sustains their apostolic fervor.

Every tertiary will feel naturally drawn to support the apostolic initiatives of the various branches of the Society of Mary (Marist Fathers, Brothers, and Sisters), which comprises their proper religious family.

The Work of the Madonna of Hope is a prayer group formed at the very heart of the Third Order of Mary since the earliest days; they pray in behalf of mothers who await their new babies and in order to obtain for these little ones the grace of Baptism.

Our Lady of Good Hope, for unborn children

Fr. Colin envisaged that even children in the womb could be brought in some way into the Marist project. The following is taken from a leaflet used in England and is intended for expectant mothers. The help of Our Lady of Good Hope is invoked. There is similar devotion in Ireland, Italy, New Zealand, and the United States.

For those who cherish the promise of new life, the time of pregnancy is a time of hope and joy.

But it is also a time of concern:
Will this birth be successful?
What will the future hold for this child?
What will life do to him/her?
And, more importantly, what will she/he do for life?

No parent is alone in these thoughts. They were the very thoughts that Mary had, as she waited the birth of Christ in hope and prayer.

Our Lady of Good Hope is a powerful help to every woman who waits in hope for the birth of a child.

Inspired by Our Lady's waiting and by her Visitation to St. Elizabeth when the unborn Saviour sanctified St. John the Baptist, this devotion places an expected child in Mary's care to obtain for it a successful birth and the grace of baptism. This devotion is part of the spiritual service offered by members of the MARIST WAY, a large group of lay people, who are part of the Marist family — a group of priests, religious and lay people in many countries of the world.

Mother and child share in the prayers and the good works of the members of this vast Marist family.

People wishing to share in this spiritual help enroll the name of the mother in a special register kept by the Director of the Third Order, and the mother and child are prayed for regularly by members of the Marist family.

The only condition of such a devotion is that the expecting parents set aside some time each day for a short prayer that the child will enjoy a safe birth and a happy future.

They should also entrust the child in a special way to the care of Mary.

An expectant Mother's daily prayer:

Lord,
I thank you for the child you have entrusted to me;
may I guard it and nourish it
as Mary looked after your Son
and brought Him into the world.
I pray you to preserve and protect this new life in me.
Give us the strength and virtue
to be good parents
that we may be worthy co-operators with you
in the formation of life.
Mary, Mother of us all,
I consecrate this child to you.
Take it under your care,
commend it to Christ your Son,
so that it may live constantly in His love.
Mary, Mother of Good Hope,
pray for us.

The Champagnat Movement of the Marist Family — a report by the Brazilian Marist Brother, Afonso Levis, F.M.S.

Up to this point, the groups describing themselves have been assisted in large measure by Marist Sisters and Fathers. The Marist Brothers of the Schools have also sponsored a movement for Marist laity, the Champagnat Movement of the Marist Family, described here below.

1. Beginnings and evolution of the Champagnat Movement of the Marist Family.

Contacts between the Marist Brothers and a great number of lay people — students, ex-students, parents, friends, fellow workers, and families — allowed for the establishment of friendly relationships down the years. A family spirit and familiarity with the spirituality of Marcellin Champagnat were already present.

Particularly since the 70's, this family spirit was the point of deeper reflection. In those days we used to speak of the "Marist Family" or of the "Greater Marist Family." This topic was taken up at the Congresses of former students held in Lyons (1974) and in Melbourne (1978). But people had very different ideas about the nature and structure of the Marist Family according to their cultures and country of origin. Even then people felt drawn toward smaller groups or local associations rather than organizations on an international level.

The 17th General Chapter of the Marist Brothers, in 1976, encouraged the participation of lay people in the Marist mission. The 18th General Chapter, in 1985, was the one to launch the Movement officially and established the basis for it in the Constitutions, in no. 164.4, in these terms:

"The Marist Family, an extension of our Institute, is a Movement for people who find themselves attracted to the spirituality of Marcellin Champagnat. In this Movement, affiliated members, young people, parents, helpers, former students, and friends deepen within themselves the spirit of our Founder so that they can live it and let it shine forth. The Institute animates and coordinates the activities of this Movement by setting up suitable structures."

In the years following the Chapter, a committee of three Brothers of the General Council and of other Brothers of various nationalities carried this reflection further on several occasions. After gathering suggestions made by Brothers and lay people in the Provinces, the committee laid down guidelines for the establishment of lay groups and for getting them underway. Finally, after another series of consultations, a booklet entitled *The Champagnat Movement of the Marist Family* was written in 1990. This document contains guidelines and principles of the movement. A circular letter, written in October 1991 by the Superior General, Brother Charles Howard, on the Champagnat Movement, places the Movement in the new theology of the laity and in contemporary ecclesiology.

2. The spirit of the Movement, its basic ideas.

The members of the Movement, following the example of Marcellin Champagnat, are animated by a "Marian and apostolic" spirituality, the main elements of which are the following:

- a deep love for Jesus Christ and a desire to be his apostles in their own milieu and their state in life;
- a love for Mary, mother and model;
- a strong and compassionate love for others, especially poor people and young people, and a great apostolic dynamism;
- a family spirit, following the example given in Nazareth, a "spirit of love characterized by simplicity and trust, joy and self-forgetfulness, forgiveness and mutual help" (*Champagnat Movement* booklet, p. 26; *Plan of Life*, no. 13);
- readiness to respond to people's needs with concrete acts;
- enthusiasm for one's work (*Champagnat Movement* booklet, p. 19; *Plan of Life*, no. 7).
- the freedom for each group to organize itself according to its members' own culture and the conditioning of their history.

3. The aims of the Movement.

The Champagnat Movement is held to be a gift from God to the Church; it is a statement in concrete terms of a call from the Holy Spirit, one which gives rise to a new thrust among lay people and inspires in them a Christian commitment according to the spirituality and charism of Marcellin Champagnat. The Champagnat Movement seeks to be a place and a way of holiness for lay people who are attracted by this way and who want to live by it and to spread it. It is a sign of hope for the Marist Brothers and for the Church.

4. How members are attracted.

"The Movement is open to any individual Christian who feels called to commit himself or herself to a closer following of Jesus, according to the spirituality of Blessed Marcellin Champagnat. To become a member of the Movement, a person makes a request to be admitted into one of the Groups. After a time of preparation, he or she is then accepted as a fully active member." (*Champagnat Movement* booklet, p. 17; *Plan of Life*, no. 6).

"A person who joins the Champagnat Movement becomes a member of a small Group, which is the basic unit of the Movement. Each group is autonomous in its own internal organization. It is the Brother Provincial or District Superior of the Marist Brothers who officially recognizes a Champagnat Movement Group in his region, or, if need be, withdraws such recognition. The major Superior may also appoint a Brother to be his liaison with the Movement and see that its spiritual life is provided for adequately." (*Champagnat Movement* booklet, p. 34; *Plan of Life*, no. 22).

Among the means for attracting and sustaining members, mention may be made of already existing groups, invitations by persons already committed, the initiative of the Brothers, courses and information on the subject, the publication of *The Champagnat Movement of the Marist Family*, and the circular letter on the Movement by the Superior General, Brother Charles Howard, as well as other favorable circumstances, for example: visits to the Hermitage, the celebration of the bicentennial of the birth of Marcellin Champagnat, the centennial of the Province, international meetings, and the like.

5. The composition of groups.

Normally, the groups are composed of 6 to 15 persons. However, some groups are more numerous, with around 25 members. Although the age of members is quite varied, adults are more numerous; there are slightly more men than women among members.

6. Procedures in the Movement.

The frequency of meetings is varied: about 50% of the groups meet every month; 20%, every week; 15%, every two weeks; 7%, every month and a half; 7%, no reply.

Besides the ordinary meetings, the fifth general gathering of the Champagnat Movement in Brazil was held at the end of January 1993, with former Brothers and their families; about 150 people took part in the three-day meeting. In France, the second Marist European Gathering took place in June 1992 with about twenty groups represented.

Normally, ordinary meetings consist of prayers, a sharing on the Gospel, reflections, information being given, celebrations, and communications on apostolic commitment.

Some groups count on the presence of Brothers; others manage by themselves.

A great majority of the lay members and of the Brothers deeply appreciated the booklet, *The Champagnat Movement of the Marist Family*, [*Plan of Life*,] which they found quite simple, open, and flexible, and which brings out the mission of the lay person. Likewise Brother Charles Howard's circular letter on the Champagnat Movement of the Marist Family has been joyfully and gratefully received.

7. Extension of the Champagnat Movement of the Marist Family.

According to the survey on the Champagnat Movement conducted as part of the preparation for the 19th General Chapter, the Movement is present in about twenty countries and has about sixty Fraternities, with a total of about 880 members (460 men and 420 women), most of whom are adults; but there are several youth groups with boys and girls. The countries with the largest numbers of groups are France (11), Spain (7), Canada (7), and Brazil (6).

The Movement aims to get stronger. This is a challenge faced with hope and daring, as we can see from what was said at the Marist European Gathering:

"Some important points have emerged which are common to us all. They are:

- the simplicity of our relationships and the friendship which unites us,

- the effort each one makes to face the difficulties in listening, in understanding one another, in remaining true to our aims,
- the prayer and reflection prevailing among us in our gatherings.

"We realized that the Group is to each of us a return to the source of Christian living, a better appreciation of Champagnat's spirit, a greater openness to others.

"These conclusions are to us clear signs of the action of the Holy Spirit, of Mary and of Champagnat in our lives.

"Our prayer is that the Holy Spirit bring to fruition these first seeds of Champagnat's inspiration and spirituality in the lives of lay people and of the Brothers.

"We also pray to the Holy Spirit to lead us, in the coming years, to take steps which could enrich us and promote mutual help between the Groups of adults and of younger people, as well as other groups inspired by the Marist ideal" (*M. Champagnat*, Bulletin n° 1, November 1992, p. 2).

Chapter 7
Historical Models of Organization and Action

Lest we be tempted to think of a single "traditional" model for the organization of the Marist laity, a brief survey of our tradition will reveal a rich variety of ways, some of which might give us a few useful ideas.

The earliest signs of life in the secular branch have left a few traces which allow brief glimpses of what they were like. We know, for example, that only two years after the early Marist aspirants left the Lyons seminary in 1816 to go into active ministry, the brother of one of them, a layman named Aloys Perrault-Maynand, appeared to identify himself as a Marist. Also at an early date, after Jean-Claude Colin became settled in his first assignment in Cerdon with his brother Pierre as pastor, the two of them gathered a group of about thirty men who met in the rectory; this was probably a forerunner of the Marist laity. And then, in 1833, a group of Marist "associates" were having meetings and retreats in Belley; Jean-Claude Colin, writing from Rome to the Marist Foundress, Mother Saint Joseph (Jeanne-Marie Chavoin), asked her to take care of them and to tell his brother Pierre and Fr. Convers to encourage and meet with them. Colin also obtained indulgences for the Belley group from the Holy See but suspended it when the Bishop of Belley expressed his concern that people would desert the cathedral, the only parish church in the town, for the Marist chapel.

More information is available on other groups, which are described here to allow us to see how they functioned.

People "Converted" during a Parish Mission

Beginning in 1825, the priests who would later be among the first Marist Fathers began preaching missions in the hill-country known as the Bugey; during the years after the formal establishment of the Society of Mary, they expanded this apostolate in the diocese of Belley and elsewhere. In the early days, particularly, they went to parishes where, since the disruption caused by the French Revolution, large numbers of people had abandoned the practice of religion. In order to sustain the perseverance of those who returned to the Church (and of those who had stayed with it) and to obtain the conversion of "sinners" (those who were still unchurched), Colin sought the Pope's approval in 1833-34 to establish the Marist confraternity during the missions and retreats he and his men were preaching.

The men and women of this confraternity would "strive by their prayers, counsel, and other better means for the conversion of sinners and the perseverance of the faithful." Every day, with simple prayers, the *Hail Mary* and the *Our Father*, they would entrust themselves and their families to Blessed Mary and pray for the conversion of sinners; they would say at least part of the rosary. They would avoid whatever might jeopardize their salvation; they would attend their group's meetings. In an age when people rarely received Communion, they would do so on all Mary's feasts and encourage their families to do likewise. From time to time, they would reflect on Mary's virtues, especially on her humility and obedience. It was a simple program accessible to anyone. Its name, "the Confraternity of Blessed Mary for the Conversion of Sinners and the Perseverance of the Faithful," reflecting its distinctively missionary thrust, was the one Colin always preferred for the secular branch of the Marists. With no other formalities and no records kept, we cannot tell how well it spread, but it was a helpful answer to a need of the times.

Young Men in a Kind of Secular Institute

In the early 1830's a certain number of young men in Lyons sought to form what we would nowadays call a secular institute. They were helped in this by Fr. Jean Cholleton, then vicar general of the diocese, earlier the seminary professor who had guided the Marist project in its planning stages (*see p. 1*). From Cholleton, they learned that the Society of Mary was to have a branch for people "living in the world," and so they became part of the Marist Third Order and called themselves the Tertiary Brothers of Mary. These dynamic young men had already entered various professions, including those of military officer, notary, lawyer, accountant, civil administrator, teacher, artist, and architect.

In answer to the need for Catholic education in Lyons, they began a school in November 1832; it was so successful that they had to move to larger premises a year later. In addition to those who lived in community and ran the school, other Tertiary Brothers lived at home but came together for regular meetings and retreats. They professed simple vows and sought to follow a hidden kind of religious life while living ostensibly as ordinary laymen in secular society. Their somewhat rigorous rule was marked by devotion to Mary as well as their dedication to numerous good works in addition to their school. It had been drawn up by their chaplain, a Marist aspirant, Father Jean-Baptiste-François Pompallier, who, in 1836, became the first missionary bishop in Western Oceania and eventually the first bishop of Auckland, New Zealand.

Between 1839 and 1841, some of their leading members joined the congregation of Marist priests, and, in the latter year, their school closed for, by then, other Catholic schools had been begun in the city. Others who also asked to become Marist priests were encouraged to continue in the lay state where, Colin said, they could do even more good. Four of the lay Marists, Dominique Meynis, Charles de Gatellier, Arthur Gabet, and Irénée Chalandon held positions of responsibility — two of them for the rest of their lives — with the Society for the Propagation of the Faith, which gave significant logistical and material support to the foreign missions.

Third Order of Mary — Fraternities of Christian Maidens, of Christian Mothers, of Men, of Young Men; Association of the Little Daughters of Mary

Early in 1836, Fr. Pompallier started a Third Order of Mary for women in Lyons by inviting Mrs. Pichot, a widow who supervised the domestic arrangements at the Tertiary Brothers' school, along with Miss Sophie David and two other women, to a meeting. They embraced a lifestyle similar to that of the men's group, emphasizing religious devotions and the practice of virtue as well as apostolic endeavors, including help for the missions in the Pacific. For a few years at least, they made private vows, as they sought to live a kind of religious life privately without leaving their social milieu.

When, in 1841, a diocesan priest in Lyons spoke from the pulpit against what he had heard about the Third Order, Colin directed that its meetings be suspended because he wanted to avoid anything that might displease the diocesan clergy. Meetings of the women's group resumed after 26 months, but two years later their director, Fr. Claude Girard, was sent to begin a new community of Marist priests in Moulins. Fr. Julien Eymard, appointed by Colin as the new director, attracted many new members. Colin, though pleased with his dynamism, was not happy with Eymard's narrower focus on "the interior life" and limitation of appeal to a spiritual elite; nevertheless, he kept Eymard as Third Order director for six years.

Eymard divided the women into two groups, those who chose not to marry (the Christian Maidens) and the "ladies" (the Christian Mothers). With a core of men who had been active in the Tertiary Brothers of Mary, he began a Fraternity for men and, soon, another for young men (in their late teens and twenties). He also brought a group of teenage girls (who had asked him to offer a Mass for their pious association) under the aegis of the Third Order and gave them the new name, "Association of the Little Daughters of Mary." For a short while, there was a fraternity for diocesan priests, but the latter, including St. Jean-Marie Vianney, the curé of Ars, were usually received individually. Affiliate groups for women were started in several towns and villages in the region around Lyons; other fraternities began in Belley, in Valbenoîte (a suburb of Saint-Étienne), in Toulon, and elsewhere.

The rules received from Pompallier, which Eymard had modified several times, were printed in a manual in 1857 by a later director, Fr. Jean-Baptiste Jacquet. These directives applied to all groups. (Though Eymard had intended to compose special rules adapted to the needs of each type of fraternity, only the Little Daughters of Mary came to have a special manual.) *The Manual of the Third Order of Mary* had the advantages of containing well-defined rules and procedures and of having printed copies available. Until the 1950's and even afterwards, it was commonly followed by most lay Marists.

Colin's ideas on the role of the secular branch of the Marist family were only dimly reflected in the printed manual. As Jan Snijders points out, Eymard and his successors "did what everyone else was doing with Third Orders: they brought together groups of pious laity who in various ways shared the spiritual life of the 'first orders.' ... Probably nothing else was possible." In fact, however, "the reality fell short of the dream."

A new dawn of Colin's "dream" for the Church and the Marist mission has come progressively with the publication of source materials by Jean Coste and Gaston Lessard and their commentaries, with the same sort of work by scholars in the other Marist branches, and with the propagation of the fundamental Marist perspective by recent general administrations and many members of the various Marist religious congregations. Colin's vision on the laity, which was rediscovered by Fr. Brendan Hayes, an Irish Marist, and which has become known and accepted only gradually, is now accessible enough to provide an orientation for the laity's participation in the Marist mission in the world of tomorrow. Some suggestions for the future will be offered in this book's final chapter.

Third Order of Mary for the Missions

Starting in 1836, with the formal approval of the Fathers' branch of the Society of Mary, successive waves of missionaries left Europe for central and western Oceania. Within ten years, women missionaries began to go, too (more about them below).

The Society for the Propagation of the Faith, based in Lyons and with lay Marist men in prominent positions of responsibility, not only saw to the providing of help for the missions abroad but also stimulated interest in them by publishing the *Annales de la Propagation de la foi*, a magazine reporting on developments and often printing letters from missionaries.

In the early days of the Marist confraternity or Third Order, the members were reminded of their association with the work of the missionaries at home and abroad through their prayers. It is not surprising then, in the context of the current missionary fervor, to hear of a project to include material help as well. In January 1845, a laywoman from Lyons spoke to the Marist missionary Bishop Jean-Baptiste Epalle before his departure for Melanesia and then to Colin of her idea for a Marist Third Order group for women "who would dedicate themselves entirely, in France, to the missions of Oceania, and would have all things in common." While we have no records to show precisely what came of this proposal, there is evidence that in 1859 at least, a Marist Fraternity for the Missions was functioning in Lyons. It apparently did not last long; by March 1861, the Christian Maidens' Fraternity in Lyons had taken over the work. At one or two work sessions every week, members prepared things needed by the missions in Oceania, and this work lasted at least through 1869. In October 1886, there was another proposal for a Third Order group who would live in community and work to send help to the Marist missions abroad.

Third Order of Mary — Women Missionaries in Oceania

Sending help from afar was not enough for some women; they became missionaries themselves. The September 1843 issue of the *Annales de la Propagation de la foi* contained a letter written by Suzanne Pukega, a recent convert on Wallis Island in the Pacific, asking that "some devout women" be sent "to teach the women of Ouvea." In answer, Françoise Perroton went — on her own initiative. She was 49 years old when, on November 15,

1845, she set sail from Le Havre with a group of Marist priests and brothers. For twenty-five years she had been active in collecting contributions for the Society for the Propagation of the Faith to use in helping the foreign missions. Now, with the encouragement of her confessor, a Capuchin priest, and a sober warning of the privations that lay ahead from the Marist Fr. Eymard, she forged ahead. At a stop in Tahiti during the long voyage, she received a letter from Eymard, who told her he had enrolled her in the Third Order of Mary. On October 25, 1846, she landed on Wallis Island to begin her life as a missionary. In August 1854, the Marist missionary Bishop Pierre Bataillon brought her to the island of Futuna, where she continued her work of education. She was consistently praised for her valuable service, her sterling character, and her patience.

Interesting details on Françoise Perroton's ministry on Futuna and Wallis Islands — beyond the scope of the present survey of organizational models — are engagingly related by Fr. Antoine Forissier in his book, *For a Marian Church: Marist Founders and Foundresses* (pp. 147-183), in which he also gives a full picture of the ten other women missionaries who went to the Pacific after Perroton (pp. 184-228).

Twelve years after Perroton's departure, other women began to follow in her footsteps. In 1857, it was decided in Lyons to accede to the requests that women should be sent to the missions in Oceania. Françoise Bartet, Marie Basset, and Jeanne Albert came forward as candidates. On November 10, 1857, they were professed as novices in the Third Order of Mary by Fr. François Yardin, Marist procurator for the missions. For the trip to the Pacific, these women were accompanied by Bishop Bataillon and some Marist Fathers also headed for the missions; on their way to board ship in England, the group stopped in Paris, where these simple lay missionaries took a vow of obedience to Bishop Bataillon and to whoever would be assigned by him to be their superior. Sailing from London on November 30, 1857, they reached Sydney, Australia, in March of the following year and in April were professed in the Third Order of Mary. On May 29, they finally reached Futuna. They had adopted a simple dress uniform as a kind of religious habit and wore the medal of the Third Order of Mary. Two days after their arrival on Futuna, Françoise Perroton was received into the Third Order (even though she had already been enrolled by Eymard, by letter, shortly after she had left France); she put on the habit her new companions had prepared for her. The following August, Fr. Victor Poupinel, the Marist visitor general for the missions, wrote a rule for the women missionaries, calling them "the Sisters of Charity of the Third Order of Mary in the Missions of Central Oceania."

In 1858, two more groups of women missionaries left France. The second group was formed by Marie Virginie Jacquier, already a member of the fraternity of the Christian Maidens in Lyons, and by Pélagie Phélippon and Clotilde Vianney, who were received as novices in the Third Order before their departure. The group sailed from London on July 27, 1858; Phélippon and Vianney were professed in the Third Order in Sydney on the following November 11. On December 2, all three arrived in New Caledonia, where, four days later, Fr. Poupinel gave them the same rule that he had given out on Futuna during the previous August.

Three women formed the third group. Jeanne Marie Autin already belonged to the Third Order Regular of Jonzieux (see next section). Marie Meissonier, who had worked at the Marist secondary school in La Seyne (a town on the Mediterranean near Toulon), had been admitted into the Third Order there by Fr. Jean-François Denis in 1856 or 1857. Jacqueline Claray-Fromage, a woman from Savoy, arrived in Lyons a month before the group's departure in October 1858 and was accepted as a novice in the Third Order. This third group arrived in Sydney on February 14, 1859, and on March 19, Miss Claray-Fromage made her profession in the Third Order of Mary. All three women finally arrived on Wallis on June 28, 1859.

The last of the "pioneers" of the Marist missionary sisters was Marie Brait, originally from Toulon. She had belonged to the

Third Order fraternity in La Seyne. When the Marist Fathers accepted her request to go to the missions, they sent her to the Marist Sisters in Belley to receive the religious and community formation which seemed necessary. Leaving London in October 1860, her ship arrived in Sydney in January 1861, and there she renewed her vow of obedience as a missionary and her consecration as a Marist on February 2. She finally arrived at her mission post in New Caledonia in March.

Evolution to the Third Order Regular of Mary and, eventually, the Missionary Sisters of the Society of Mary

These "pioneers" (as the Missionary Sisters of the Society of Mary, their successors, call them) left for Oceania as lay women, ordinary members of the Third Order of Mary. The religious dress they wore and the vow of obedience they took before leaving indicated, however, that they wanted to belong to a religious congregation. For almost twenty-five years, there was a clear evolution towards a more authentically religious form of life until the time when the Third Order Regular for the Missions of Oceania was erected canonically, with the status of a diocesan congregation in Wallis, and a house of formation was opened in France.

While the Sisters committed themselves by the three vows of religion, they were still dependent on the vicars apostolic in the missions; among themselves, there was no superior, properly so called. For fifty years, the Third Order Regular of Mary functioned in this way. Finally, on December 30, 1931, by a decree of the Sacred Congregation for the Propagation of the Faith, the congregation became a true religious institute of pontifical right, the Missionary Sisters of the Society of Mary, with its own constitutions and the whole internal organization proper to the religious life.

Other forms of a Third Order Regular of Mary

Because Colin always looked upon the secular branch of Marists as "an immense association which will envelop the whole world," he envisioned its having several branches for people living in varied situations. As early as 1838, he spoke of the possibility of some members "who would want to live a more retired life." In 1843, he said that it might include "men and women under vows," even though this would not be the case for most, for it would also have "married people." In addressing the Marist Fathers' policy-making body (general chapter) in 1866, he said that the Third Order should include a "regular" branch whose members would live in community with a religious habit. And he returned to the same idea in 1872 and in the Constitutions written under his direction for the lay confraternity. Eymard, too, proposed in 1846 and in 1854 the establishment for a house for Third-Order members who might want to live in community. In 1886, Léon Besson put forth a plan for a Third Order regular under the aegis of the ordinary Third Order of Mary.

All these projects, it should be noted, were not intended as a pattern for all members but for a smaller number, those "who would wish to lead a life more like that of vowed religious." The Marist women who went to Oceania as missionaries, we have just seen, followed this course in forming a Third Order Regular of Mary, which eventually became a religious congregation in the full canonical sense. Two other cases may be noted.

Third Order Regular of Mary in Jonzieux

In Jonzieux, a village south of Saint-Étienne, a Third Order Regular of Mary was founded in 1854 by Fr. Richard, pastor of the parish, with four local women, one of whom, Jeanne Marie Autin, later went to Oceania as a missionary. Another member, Miss Couturier, was later a missionary in Oceania as well. A membership list dated 1856 has fifteen names. They took vows, lived in community, and wore a habit like the one adopted by the missionary sisters. Their first profession of vows, at least, was authorized by Cardinal de Bonald, the Archbishop of Lyons; a Marist priest, Fr. Louis Touche, presided.

These sisters were devoted to the care of old women who lived alone and were sick or disabled; the sisters took them in at their house; they visited and gave help to sick people in their homes and offered many other services in the parish. So as to provide for the material needs of the community and of the rather numerous boarders to whom they gave shelter, a few of them made velvet ribbons on their small low-warp looms, while others did sewing. They also had an apostolate to the young girls of the parish, and they directed a women's choir.

Little Servants of Nazareth

The Little Servants of Nazareth (in French, *Petites Servantes de Nazareth*), founded by Fr. Alexandre Billion, a Marist priest, and Marcelle Charrion (Sister Marie de la Trinité) in 1922, began with some women of the Third Order of Mary in Lyons. Its specific apostolate was to provide domestic service in communities of both diocesan and religious priests. Marie-Andréa Triviot (Sister Marie de la Miséricorde) was for a long time its superior. In addition to providing service at the Marist houses in La Neylière, Belley, Morhange (Moselle), Lyons, Sainte-Foy-lès-Lyon, Riom, and Toulon, the Sisters also served at diocesan retreat houses in Lyons and in Oran (Algeria), as well as in the minor seminary and archbishop's residence in Lyons. This Third Order regular became a congregation of diocesan right in 1947. The institute's constitutions professed a spirit identical to what Colin had laid down for the Society of Mary, with emphasis on the hidden life of Nazareth, applied to humble and hidden service to the priesthood. Difficulties in recruitment led the Sisters to ask to be united with the Marist Sisters, and this took place in September 1968.

Incorporating existing associations into the Marist Laity

The idea of making an existing pious organization into a Marist Third Order or confraternity first occurred in the academic year 1816-17, when Fr. Jean-Claude Courveille, one of the original planners of the Marist project, was in the French town of Verrières. An association of the Holy Family had been begun at the local seminary, and Courveille had sought — unsuccessfully — to have it become "the Third Order of the Maryists." Another instance occurred in Lyons in November 1846, when some teenage girls, who called themselves the Servants of Mary, were associated with the Third Order of Mary by Eymard under the new name of Little Daughters of Mary.

Colin, who strongly favored the participation of lay Marists in the religious services and pious works of parishes, apparently brought up a similar idea in a conversation with Father Carton, the pastor of Saint-Pierre in the Montrouge district of Paris, when the latter visited him in La Neylière. Carton later reported, "In the mind of the founder, the Third Order was not supposed to be restricted the way it is today. The Very Reverend Father Founder would have wanted the parish's congregations and associations to become part of it." As Marist Father Alphonse Cozon explained, it might be easier and more acceptable to pastors to impart the Marist spirit to existing parochial organizations rather than "laboriously creating a nucleus of persons who would perforce necessarily be removed from existing works."

Something analogous occurred recently in Mexico when the Marist spirit was presented to existing Apostolic Groups. They adopted it and thus became what they call the "Marist Family" (*see pp. 129-130*).

The Catechists of Mary, in Paris

Alphonse Cozon, a Marist priest who, in his younger days, had had long conversations on the Marist lay branch with Jean-Claude Colin and had written them down almost verbatim, was given charge of most of the fraternities of the Third Order of Mary in Paris in 1906. It soon happened that one of the women's fraternities changed the time for its meetings and two members told him they had to withdraw because at this new time they were already committed to teaching catechism in their parish. Cozon saw this as a call from Providence and immediately sought and obtained authorization to organize a new "Apostolic Fraternity," soon renamed the "Fraternity of Catechists." From the very beginning, Miss Françoise de la Rupelle, a Marist, was not only a dedicated catechist but helped Cozon in the organization of the group. They had two aims: (1) to recruit women catechists to give religious instruction to the children of poor people, and (2) to give to the catechists themselves a continuing spiritual formation which alone could assure the supernatural effectiveness of their apostolate and their perseverance in it. A daily time for mental prayer was an important part of their way of life.

The group grew and developed until 1912, when it was made independent of the Third Order and, under the name "Catechists of Mary," began to admit people who did not belong to the Third Order of Mary. Miss de la Rupelle pioneered an out-reach to children and adolescents who did not come to the parochial catechetical centers. She and other Catechists of Mary made contact with non-practicing — and often unbaptized — children in hospitals and even on the street, set out to win the confidence of the children and their families, and went to their homes and even workplaces to give religious instruction. After 1919, its members became part of the Parisian Archconfraternity for Catechists. Cozon continued as the catechists' spiritual advisor until 1922 when, at the age of 83, he could go no more.

Chapter 8
Foreword to the Future

Jean-Claude Colin dreamed of "the whole world Marist." How can we advance toward that ideal? Here are a few thoughts for looking forward to the future, the Marist future.

Remember the broad picture of the Marist project: not only priests and other vowed religious, but all the People of God. Those believers other than clerics or religious are essential in the "work of Mary"; without them, the Marists are incomplete.

The hallmark is the Marist spirit, and Mary is a person with whom Marists develop a special relationship. She leads them surely to Jesus, her son.

All Marists are missionary in character. They want to win people over to God and the body of believers, but they go about it in Mary's gentle way: they pray; they work in a "hidden" way; they don't care for show or credit; they're unthreatening. In countless different ways, they are intent upon evangelizing a world that hears so little of the Good News of Jesus Christ; they are catholic (universal) in their outlook and in their out-reach. Marists — those living in secular society as well as the religious — are living in a secularized world suffering from too much emptiness and desolation: this is the world toward which they have a special mission.

Marist religious are not trying to draw lay Marists into a pre-set agenda but are coming to understand that they are to assist the laity in *their* mission. The role of Marist religious is to serve, not to dictate; it is to nourish the Marist laity with the spirit of Mary, to help in the formation of lay Marists in Mary's way.

The Marist laity is not so much an organization you join as an identity you take on. It is a school for the spirit by which you gradually become "the work of Mary" (*see p. 60*). To those who want to draw new people into the Marist family, we would say: Seek to involve those who are already most active; they may well appreciate that subtle dimension which the Marist way can add to their lives. Look also to people who are confined by infirmity or old age; they may well be enriched by the Marist spirit and they would greatly enrich the Marist family by their prayer. Look to anyone you know or might come to know; each person is precious in the eyes of the Mother of Jesus.

While the Marist laity is not essentially an organization, lay Marists usually do organize, though in many different ways. They have meetings and retreats: for mutual support and to have a channel for learning — and being reminded of — the Marist spirit and the Christian life and mission.

Some lay Marists do live apart from the others; they live too far from an organized group or they've moved away from where they got started. Often enough, however, they serenely approach others to gather with them "under the mantle of Mary" and begin to form new Marist groups where there were none before. A Marist religious is not always available on the spot; but one may be able to advise, encourage, and help from afar with only an occasional visit.

Some new Marist groups start "from scratch," from a chance encounter with lay Marists or with a Marist religious. Sometimes, an already-existing apostolic group learns of the Marist spirit — perhaps through a retreat — and its members adopt it and their group becomes a Marist group.

A wide variety of forms is what the Marist founders, particularly Colin, intended; and now, at the end of the twentieth century, many different forms of Marist laity are developing. Older forms are surviving and being refreshed by the infusion of Colin's insights - and this includes the form known as the Third Order of Mary, which evolved since the 1830's under the guidance of people like Pompallier, Eymard, and Jacquet. This Third Order should be maintained and fostered as one of the ways of being Marist, though it is certainly not the only way.

What distressed Colin about the way in which the Third Order developed was that it was too "restricted": in his day, its limitation to a certain type of membership, with a rule largely uniform for all members, unduly curbed the universal extension that was part of his prophetic vision of "the whole world Marist." The lesson for today is this: Do not restrict the development of the Marist laity by insisting on one form only.

If your Marist identity is of value to you, share it. Invite new people to become Marists, but invite in a warmhearted way; never badger like an obnoxiously desperate salesman.

If a group gets quite large, its members may lose their sense of belonging; it may be time to divide into two or more smaller groups. Smaller groups may be more eager to attract new members. Members should be wary of any tendency to close in on themselves and to stop inviting strangers.

Launching new Marist groups — whether of a type already existing in the country or of a new type — contributes toward making "the whole world Marist." We've seen in chapter 6 several alternate ways in which a new group can begin, and these are but random examples.

In the early days (back in the 1830's and 1840's), there were distinct groups for men. In the present-day situation, it may happen that some men will be reluctant to become part of a group whose members are mostly women. In the case of a large group, a sub-group for men occasionally or usually meeting separately may meet the need. In some circumstances, it may be a good idea to have an autonomous men's group.

In Colin's mind, Marist confraternities were to be established in places where there were no Marist religious. This was to be the normal pattern though he did allow for groups near Marist religious communities. If the proportions have been reversed over the years, the time has come to restore the balance by starting Marist groups in new places. With lay initiative and leadership this becomes quite possible. In some parts of the world, groups begun by lay Marists have flourished for many years. Other groups, begun around Marist religious, have seen the Sisters or Brothers or priests relinquish the ministry which kept them there, but the lay Marist groups have continued to prosper with their lay leadership.

In your country or region, whenever there seems to be a call for — or a need for — a new kind of lay Marist group, be ready and willing to launch one.

The development of other Marist groups with a structure or emphasis different from your own is a cause for rejoicing. Each type (new or old) is an enrichment of the Marist family. The members of each type do well to treasure their own particular emphasis even as they think well of other groups who live their Marist spirit in another way. On occasion, perhaps once a year or every two or three years, it would be an excellent thing for the different kinds of groups to come together for a retreat or a congress for the celebration of their common Marist identity.

Because a personal relationship with Mary and, through her, with Jesus, is a significant part of the spirit Marists embrace, it stands to reason that personal relationships with other Marists are important. (Most of us have come into Mary's family through personal contact with a Marist.) Retreats and congresses are occasions for sharing, for communication. The one obligation Colin placed on Marist religious in regard to the Marist laity is the communication of the Marist spirit. Regional animators for the Marist laity do this, in part, through their newsletters and visits.

Much has been left unsaid in this little book — about the limitless love of God for each of us, about the gift of faith, about the extraordinary powers given in baptism for the good of the Church. This book, essentially introductory in scope, has said a little about Jesus and his mother Mary, about being graciously chosen, about the spirit of Mary and the work of Mary, about the simple, attainable, open, catholic ways of ordinary Catholics who become Marists. We have seen how they accept the mission to be "like a bridge" to people who do not believe, to those who do not practice the faith, to those whose faith (like their own, like anyone's) is strengthened by the support of other people. But this book is not the final word; it is only a foreword to a future in the family of Mary.

Sources

Works Cited and Suggestions for Further Reading

See pp. 176-184 for documentation notes.

Works cited by an abbreviated title:

AT = *Antiquiores textus constitutionum Societatis Mariae.* Ed. Jean Coste et al. 7 fascicles. Rome, 1955.

Const. SM 1872 = *Constitutions of the Society of Mary: Latin text in Conformity with the Text Approved by the General Chapter of 1872 with English Translation.* Rome, 1992.

Const. SM 1987 = *Constitutions of the Society of Mary* [1987]. Rome, 1988.

FA = *A Founder Acts: Reminiscences of Jean-Claude Colin.* By Gabriel-Claude Mayet. Ed. Jean Coste. Trans. William Joseph Stuart and Anthony Ward. Rome, 1983.

FS = *A Founder Speaks: Spiritual Talks of Jean-Claude Colin.* Ed. Jean Coste. Trans. Anthony Ward. Rome, 1975.

LMA = *Lay Marists: Anthology of Historical Sources.* Ed. Charles Girard. Rome, 1993.

OM = *Origines maristes.* Ed. Jean Coste and Gaston Lessard. 4 vols. Rome, 1960-1967.

Works cited by author (and title):

Boudon, H. M. *Dieu seul ou association pour l'intérêt de Dieu seul.* Paris, 1662; rpt. 1809.

Coste, Jean. *Lectures on Society of Mary History (Marist Fathers).* Rome 1965.

Coste, Jean. "Le mandat donné par ses compagnons à Marcellin Champagnat en 1816: Essai d'histoire de la tradition." *L'étude de la spiritualité mariste — The Study of Marist Spirituality*. Colloquium. Rome, 1984. 1-16.

_________. *Marie, aujourd'hui chez les pères maristes. The Place of Mary among Marists Today*. S.M. Document 1. Rome 1973.

_________. "The Marist Spirit and the Third Order of Mary," *Acta S.M.*, 7 (1963-1967): 188-194. (Reprinted in *Congress of the Third Order of Mary*. Rome, 1964.)

_________. "Mary in the Newborn Church and at the End of Time." Colloquium, Rome, 1992. To be published.

_________. "Piccole Ancelle di Nazareth." *Dizionario degli istituti di perfezione*. Vol. 6, pp. 1584-1585.

_________. "The Role of Mary at the Birth of the Church and at the End of Time," *Acta S.M.* 5 (1959), 263-281; 419-451; 6 (1960), 53-87; 179-197.

_________. *The Spirit of the Society: Historical Commentary on the Constitutions of the Marist Fathers, nn. 49-50*. Trans. S. Fagan. Rome, 1963. (First published in *Acta S.M.* 6 (1960-1962): 445-533, 581-677.)

_________. *Third Order Conference*. Mimeographed. Rome, 1979.

Delumeau, Jean. *Rassurer et protéger: Le sentiment de sécurité dans l'Occident d'autrefois*. Paris: Fayard, 1989.

Doohan, Leonard. "Lay People and the Church," *The Way: Review of Contemporary Christian Spirituality*. 32 (1992): 168-177.

Forissier, Antoine. *For a Marian Church: Marist Founders and Foundresses*. Trans. Jessica Leonard. Middlegreen: St. Paul Publications, 1992.

Frappi, Renato. "Un nuovo gruppo di laici maristi." *Maria: Mensile sulle opere e sulle missioni dei padri maristi,* novembre-dicembre 1992 (n. 11-12): 22-23.

Hever, Jim. *Marist Values in Education*. Thesis for Master of Education. Trinity College, Dublin, 1991.

Jago, John. *Mary Mother of Our Hope*. [Circular letter] N. 163 - X, 1. Rome, 24 September 1986.

John Paul II. *Post-Synodal Apostolic Exhortation* Christifideles Laici *of His Holiness John Paul II on the Vocation and the Mission of the Lay Faithful in the Church and in the World*. Dublin: Veritas Publications, 1989.

Keel, Edwin. "Clergy/Laity Turnabout." Unpublished paper. Rome, 1992.

________. "Jean-Claude Colin: Poet and Prophet — A Study of the Symbolic and Mythic Elements in his Language." *L'étude de la spiritualité mariste — The Study of Marist Spirituality.* Colloquium. Rome, 1984. 143-193.

Larkin, Craig. *A Certain Way.* (To be published.)

Marcel, Gabriel. "On the Ontological Mystery." *The Philosophy of Existentialism.* New York: Citadel Press, 1956. 9-46.

McKay, Frank. *The Marist Laity: Finding the Way Envisaged by Father Colin.* Maristica 4. Rome, 1991.

Mijolla, Marie Cécile de. *Origins in Oceania: Missionary Sisters of the Society of Mary, 1845-1931.* Rome, 1980.

Perrone Pacifico, Nicola. "Marist Spirituality: A Layperson's Comment." *Intercom S.M.* July-September 1987 (no. 3): 11-12.

Ryan, Bernard J. *Where Does Creative Fidelity Call Us?* (Superior General's Report to 25th General Chapter), N. 162 - IX, 5; 29 June 1985.

Sérol, Maurice. "Le Rév. P. Alphonse Cozon." *Physionomies maristes d'un premier siècle, 1836-1936.* Mimeographed. Rome, 1935.

Snijders, Jan. *The Age of Mary.* Maristica 1. Rome, 1988.

Documentation of Sources and Citations

Abbreviated titles or authors' names (and brief titles) given here;

for full listing, see pp. 173-175.

Foreword

Image: "like a bridge"

Colin's remarks on February 6, 1872: OM 3, doc. 846, § 36; LMA, doc. 334, § 36.

Marie Elisabeth Blot, letters of December 4, 1868, and February 6, 1869: LMA, docs. 310, § 6; 313, § 10.

Citation from Fr. Edwin Keel, S.M.: "Clergy/Laity Turnabout," unpublished paper, Rome 1992.

Chapter 1

Origin of the idea:

Jean Coste, *Lectures on Society of Mary History*, pp. 15-30; Coste, *Third Order Conference* (1979), pp. 1-4.

"Support of the new-born Church; ... at the end of time": FS, doc. 4 (OM 2, doc. 422). See the studies by Coste: "The Role of Mary at the Birth of the Church and at the End of Time," *Acta S.M.*, 5 (1959): 273-281; and "Mary in the Newborn Church and at the End of Time," Colloquium (Rome, 1992, to be published). See also the texts in OM, docs. 482; 582; 631; 674; 690; 752, § 43 *in fine*; 802, § 1.

The Marist aspirants' pledge of 1816: OM 1, doc. 50; see also: Coste, *Lectures*, pp. 30-33.

Like the branches of a tree:

OM 2, docs. 425, § 12; 591, § 2; OM 3, docs. 874, § 4; also FS, docs. 2, § 2. See also Coste, *Lectures*, pp. 21, 28-29; OM 2, docs. 499, addition *l*, note 2; 574, § 1; OM 3, doc. 819, § 7, note 3; H. M. Boudon, *Dieu seul ou association pour l'intérêt de Dieu seul*.

Inclusion of teaching Brothers among the branches: OM 1, doc. 416, § 1; OM 2, doc. 757, § 2; and Jean Coste, "Le mandat donné par ses compagnons à Marcellin Champagnat en 1816," in *The Study of Marist Spirituality*, pp. 2-3.

The branch of Marists living in secular society: LMA, doc. 9, § 109; AT, fasc. 1, p. 83.

Plan of the Society of Mary presented to the Holy See in 1832-1833: LMA, docs. 7, § 6; 9, § 5; 11; 12. The secular branch is described in LMA, docs. 8; 9, § 109-113, 127; and 13. See also Coste, *Lectures*, pp. 96-101.

Blessing of the secular branch with grants of indulgences: LMA, docs. 19, 20, 21, 22; see Coste, *Lectures*, pp. 99-100; and Coste, *Third Order Conference* (1979), pp. 15-16.

The secular branch — Whole world Marist:

LMA, doc 334, § 36; FS, doc. 1, § 1 (LMA, doc. 39, § 1).

Marist family open to all through its lay branch: FS, doc. 2 (LMA, doc. 41), § 2 and note 3.

On Colin's idea and his insistence on it: See LMA, docs. 6, § 7; 327, § 3; 334, § 18; 335, § 46; 392, § 1; 395, § 1.

Diocesan clergy included in the secular branch:

Provisions for diocesan priests-members: LMA, doc. 9, § 112; 13, § 3, 7 (nos. 8 & 9); 395, § 25.

Diocesan priests-members: Carton, LMA, doc. 441, § 28; 475, § 7; 479, § 13. *Dupuy*, LMA, doc. 94. *Vianney*, LMA, doc. 75, § 2; 81, § 1-5; 121, § 1; 156, § 5; 255; 468, § 32, 39. *A Marist fraternity of diocesan priests in Lyons*, LMA, doc. 245, § 11; 464, § 2.

Name:

The name of Mary: LMA, doc. 335, § 61.

Third Order: In July-August 1833: LMA, docs. 6; 7; 8; 10. — In letter of December 14, 1833: LMA, doc. 10. Compare with petition to the Holy See: LMA, doc. 9, § 5 (December 1833), where the "confraternity of lay people living in the world," no longer called a third order, is listed with the "orders" of priests, Brothers, and Sisters. — In 1850 confirmation: LMA, doc. 170.

Marist lay confraternity or association — in 1834 and 1874: LMA, docs. 19; 20; 21; 395, § 5, 7.

Not a third order (1874): LMA, doc. 335, § 47.

Understanding of the terms "lay" and "laity": Snijders, *The Age of Mary*, p. 112; Doohan, pp. 168-177, especially pp. 168-170. Vatican II documents cited in Doohan's article and in this chapter: Dogmatic constitution on the Church (*Lumen gentium*), 31.1, 13.3, 40.3; and pastoral constitution on the Church in the modern world (*Gaudium et spes*), 36.

Chapter 2

The testimonies given in chapter 2 were written, for the most part, by lay Marists and a few diocesan priests in answer to a request made by Fr. Laurence Duffy, the International Animator for the Marist Laity. Two of them came from published sources:

Renato Frappi, S.M., "Un nuovo gruppo di laici maristi," *Maria: Mensile sulle opere e sulle missioni dei padri maristi*, novembre-dicembre 1992 (n. 11-12): 22-23.

Nicola Perrone Pacifico, "Marist Spirituality: A Layperson's Comment," *Intercom S.M.*, July-September 1987 (no. 3), pp. 11-12.

Chapter 3

The "Whole World Marist":

LMA, docs. 16, § 9; 47, § 2 (OM, docs. 304, § 9; 427, § 2); LMA, doc. 248, § 3.

Among the aims of the Lay Branch: LMA, 9, § 109; "of one heart and one mind": Acts 4:32.

New Church: LMA, doc. 114, § 1 (FS, doc. 120; OM, doc. 632).

Sharing in the same spirit: LMA, docs. 335, § 47; 395, § 9; 431, § 14, 20, 30-31, 35; 474, § 9; 476, § 6; 481, § 7.

Spirit:

Colin to Cozon: MLA, doc. 335, § 4.

Colin's circular letter of April 1, 1842: cited in Coste, *The Spirit of the Society*, p. 624.

Key text: Spirit of the Society in SM Constitutions: Const. SM 1872, nos. 49-50 (repeated in Const. SM 1987, no. 228).

Coste's conclusion on the Marist spirit: Coste, *The Spirit of the Society*, p. 677.

Coste's discussion of Marist spirit: Coste, *The Spirit of the Society*, pp. 475-479, 677. Coste, "The Marist Spirit and the Third Order of Mary," p. 189.

Basic Points of Reference:

Coste, "The Marist Spirit and the Third Order of Mary," pp. 189-192.

How Marists Relate to Mary:

Coste, *The Place of Mary among Marists Today*, pp. 6-12, 36. [Translation modified to bring it closer to the French.]

The Place of Mary among Marists:

Coste, *The Spirit of the Society*, pp. 481-483; Coste, *The Place of Mary among Marists Today*, pp. 10-14; Coste, *Lectures on Society of Mary History*, pp. 144-151.

Basic Orientation of the Lay Marists:

The "statement intended for lay people": The lay Confraternity's Constitutions (translation): LMA, doc. 395.

Confraternity's Constitutions written by Fr. Jean Jeantin from notes and oral explanations which Colin gave him; among "notes" were two articles written in 1868 by Fr. Georges David on Colin's direction:

De Societatis spiritu [*The Spirit of the Society*], Fathers' Constitutions (1872), nos. 49-50, in AT, fasc. 5, p. 28; in 1992 edition, pp. 34-37. *Du culte que les membres de la Société doivent rendre à la Sainte Vierge* [*The Devotion which Members of the Society Should Have toward the Blessed Virgin*], in AT, fasc. 4, pp. 51-53 (cf. notes in AT, fasc. 4, pp. 8-9; AT, fasc. 5, p. 7).

"every excellent and perfect gift...": James 1: 17; citation from LMA, doc. 395, § 30.

For background, see: LMA, docs. 365, introd.; 373, § 2; 425, § 2; 474: § 22, note 19; § 44, note 28; § 55, note 29.

The Marist Way and Mission:

Coste, *The Place of Mary among Marists Today*, p. 34.

Images:

A Tree with Its Branches: LMA, docs. 76, § 2; 126, § 2-5; 185, § 3-4; 232, § 37, 39; 323, § 10; 437, § 6; 454, § 4.

Vine and branches: John 15:5. (See also sources for chapter 1.)

A Barque or Small Sailing Ship: (Skiff, *nacelle*): LMA, doc. 245, § 35, 37. — (Barque): LMA, docs. 305, § 1, 12-13; 313, § 6; 354, § 1; 357, § 5; 376, § 10. — (Little ship, *navicula*): LMA, doc. 392, § 1.

A Bridge: (see sources for foreword, *Image: "like a bridge"*).

The Virgin Mary Wearing a Mantle: Colin: LMA, doc. 83, § 2 (FS, doc. 78, § 2). — Maîtrepierre: LMA, doc. 226, § 66. — Cozon: LMA, doc. 474, § 30. — (Cf. Mayet: LMA, doc. 439, § 56).

Jean Delumeau, "La Vierge au grand manteau," chapter VII, in his book, *Rassurer et protéger: Le sentiment de sécurité dans l'Occident d'autrefois*, pp. 261-289.

Themes Studied in a Course for Lay Marists:

Gracious Choice: Const. SM 1872, no. 49.

"Where does the phrase ... come from?" Phrase written in 1868 by Fr. Georges David, from the sentences dictated by Colin: See Coste, *The Spirit of the Society*, pp. 493-495, 499, 617-619, 647 (also in *Acta S.M.* 6, same page numbers). For biographies of Marist founders, see: Forissier, *For a Marian Church: Marist Founders and Foundresses*.

(citation on pp. 69-70): McKay, p. 60; McKay cites article in *Fraternités maristes*, avril 1988.

See also: Coste, *The Spirit of the Society*, pp. 619-624, 635-636, 647-650.

"Support of the new-born Church; ... at the end of time": FS, doc. 4; OM 2, doc. 422; FS, docs. 117, § 3; 120, § 1. (See also sources for chapter 1, *Origin of the idea*).

(citation from Colin on p. 73): FS, doc. 117, § 3.

Hidden and Unknown in This World: "unknown and indeed even hidden in this world," Const. SM 1872, no. 50; Const. SM 1987, no. 228.

(citation from Colin on p. 75): OM, doc. 819, § 122.

(citation on p. 76): Snijders, p. 106.

(citation from SM 1874 Const. on p. 78): Const. SM 1987, no. 24.

(citation from Colin on p. 78): FS, doc. 115, § 7.

"Think as Mary, judge as Mary, feel and act as Mary in all things": Const. SM 1872, no. 49.

The section, "**Feelings are personal**" (pp. 80-81), is based on a dissertation by Jim Hever, S.M., *Marist Values in Education*.

The section, "**If we don't imitate Mary**" (p. 82), is based largely on Coste, *The Spirit of the Society*, p. 655.

Chapter 4

Whole chapter based on: John Paul II, *Post-Synodal Apostolic Exhortation* Christifideles Laici (Dublin: Veritas Publications, 1989).

The First Step: *Christifideles Laici*, nos. 34, 35.

Life according to the Holy Spirit: *Christifideles Laici*, no. 16.

Living One's Vocation: Citation from St. Leo: *Christifideles Laici*, no. 58.

Chapter 5

Creative Fidelity:

Marcel, pp. 35-36; Ryan, pp. 3-4; also, Snijders, pp. 2-18.

Becoming a Marist:

The name Marist: See sources for chapter 1, *Name.*

Various identifications of "Marist" people: LMA, doc. 301, § 4; McKay, p. 130.

Who may become a member? LMA, doc. 395, § 10; also, LMA, doc. 9, § 109.

Formalities of membership: LMA, docs. 8, § 5 (1); 9, § 110; 395, § 25; McKay, p. 130. LMA, doc. 395, § 13; see also LMA, doc. 376, § 5. LMA, doc. 395, § 28.

Structures and Rules: LMA, docs. 47, § 6; 395; 431, § 31.

Local Leadership:

Role of "directors," "servants, not masters": LMA, doc. 431, § 18, 31, 39.

"shine out into the Church": LMA, doc. 431, § 20.

Practices:

"Missionaries of action and of prayer": Citation from Colin on p. 108: FS, doc. 190, § 3.

Early lists of simple devotional practices: LMA, docs. 9, § 110-113; 13, § 1-3; 47, § 6.

Devotion to Mary in the Confraternity's 1874 Constitutions: LMA, doc. 395, § 29-40.

Apostolate and Evangelization:

Missionary thrust in early documents: LMA, docs. 11, § 7; 13, § 1, 4 (1); see also doc. 395, § 5, 7.

Early 19th cent. apostolates: LMA, docs. 26, § 21; 57, § 2; 73; 437.

Giving preference to diocesan and parochial works: LMA, docs. 132, § 37; 159, § 13; 173, § 5; 244, § 10; 284, § 43, 68; 335, § 69; 395, § 16; 408, § 4; 431, § 27-29; 468, § 31; 472, § 11; 474, § 60, 82; 481, § 4.

Variety of Organizational Structures:

Acts 4:32, "of one heart and one mind," as the ideal: LMA, docs. 9, § 109; 47, § 2; 151, § 10; 173, § 20; 174, § 74; 245, § 30; 273, § 8; 284, § 31; 309, § 2; 431, § 29; 435, § 8.

Diversity of forms, in statements by Colin: LMA, docs. 47, § 6; 70, § 1; 75, § 5; 91, § 1; 113, § 2; 301, § 2; 331, § 1-3; 332, § 3-8, 14; 335, § 60-61; 395, § 10-11.

Colin's objection to Third Order as "too circumscribed": LMA, doc. 408, § 5

Chapter 6

The testimonies given in chapter 6 were written, for the most part, by lay Marists and a few diocesan priests, in answer to a request made by Fr. Laurence Duffy, the International Animator for the Marist Laity. Some of them came from (or drew upon) published sources:

Parish Pastoral Support Team, Fiji: Michael Bransfield, S.M., "New Pastoral Initiative in Fiji," *Intercom S.M.*, June-September 1989 (no. 3), p. 12.

Marie-Jeunesse, Québec, Canada: François Grossin, S.M., "Marie-Jeunesse: une manière de vivre," *Intercom S.M.*, October-December 1989 (no. 4), p. 4.

Marianisches Apostolat, Germany: Bernd Kordes, S.M., "Dritter Orden Mariens / Marianisches Apostolat," *Marianisches Apostolat*, Heft 13: November 1992, pp. 23-28.

Marist Spirituality Groups, Third Order of Mary, Italy: Citation from Fr. Colin: FS, doc. 120, § 1; LMA, doc. 114, § 1.

The Champagnat Movement of the Marist Family:

Brother Charles Howard, *The Champagnat Movement of the Marist Family*, Circular, Rome, vol. XXIX, October 15, 1991, no. 7, pp. 337-414.

Champagnat Movement of the Marist Family, Rome, 16 July 1990; reprinted (with numbered paragraphs) under the title, *Plan of Life*, at the end of the Circular of October 15, 1991.

M. Champagnat, Rome, Bulletin n° 1, Nov. 1992; n° 2, Jan. 1993.

Survey on the Champagnat Movement of the Marist Family, preparatory to the 19th General Chapter, 1993.

Chapter 7

Beginnings of the Lay "Associates" or Confraternity:

Early signs of life: LMA, docs. 1; 2; 60; 226, § 60; 455; 456; 460.

Cerdon: LMA, docs. 60, 455, 456, 460.

Belley (1832): LMA, docs. 10, § 11; 11, § 6; 12, § 11; 457; 458, § 1-3; 459, § 2. Indulgences granted to Belley group: LMA, docs. 19, 20, 21. Suspended, but begun again (after August 1839): LMA, docs. 47, § 3, § 8; 55.

On the early history of the Marist Laity: Coste, *Third Order Conference*, pp. 1-20; Frank McKay, *The Marist Laity*, pp. 2-56; and also the introductions to the four parts of LMA.

People "Converted" during a Parish Mission: LMA, doc. 13, § 1-2, 4.

Young Men in a Kind of Secular Institute:

Lyons 1832 — Tertiary Brothers of Mary: LMA, docs. 3; 4; 5; 99, § 27; 414, § 38; 415.

Their history: LMA, docs. 26; 234, § 3-8; 414; 415, § 1-11; 437.

Professional background of members: LMA, doc. 415, § 2-3.

Their rule: LMA, docs. 14 and 15.

Blessed with grants of indulgences: LMA, docs. 29, 30, 31, 32.

Third Order of Mary — various Fraternities in Lyons:

Early history: LMA, docs. 34; 35; 234; 245; 415, § 12-13.

Suspension of meetings, Nov. 1841 - Sept. 1843: LMA, doc. 74.

Rules of the Third Order of Mary: Revision by Eymard (1847): LMA, doc. 132. Manual (1st ed., 1857): LMA, docs. 283; 284; Manual (9th ed., 1937, in French); English trans. of Manual (eighth ed., 1926; rpt. 1954). Manual of the Little Daughters of Mary (2nd ed., 1879): LMA, doc. 422.

Critique (at conclusion of this section): Snijders, p. 102.

Third Order of Mary for the Missions:

Missionary aim of lay confraternity in 1833-34; prayers for the missions in Oceania: LMA, docs. 13, § 1; 40, § 3; 74, § 8.

Proposal of a Third Order for the Missions in 1845: LMA, doc. 85, § 2-6.

Fraternity for the Missions, in 1859: LMA, doc. 290, § 3.

Christian Maidens' work for the missions (1861-1869): LMA, docs. 292, § 9; 293, § 8; 294, § 7; 295, § 6; 312, § 6.

1886 project for helping the Marist missions: LMA, doc. 451, § 8.

Third Order of Mary — Women Missionaries in Oceania:

Letter from Suzanne Pukega: Annales de la Propagation de la foi, 15 (1843), 415-416; partial citation in LMA, doc. 108, introd.

Françoise Perroton: Mijolla, pp. 37-43; LMA, doc. 108.

The other "pioneer" women missionaries following Perroton: Mijolla, pp. 47-69; LMA, docs. 286; 287; 288; 289.

Details on Perroton: Forissier, pp. 147-183. *Details on other early women missionaries:* Forissier, pp. 184-228.

Third Order Regular of Mary; Missionary Sisters of the Society of Mary: Mijolla, p. 279; see also pp. 183-269.

Other forms of a Third Order Regular of Mary:

Colin's ideas: LMA, doc. 334, § 18. LMA, docs. 47, § 6; 75, § 5; 301, § 2; 331, § 1, 3; 332, § 14; 376, § 4; 395, § 12, Also, LMA, docs. 113, § 2; 408, § 4; 474, § 39.

Proposals by Eymard and Léon Besson: LMA, docs. 100, § 7; 255, § 9; 451, § 4, 10.

Third Order Regular of Mary in Jonzieux: LMA, docs. 267; 288; 289, § 1, 4, 8-10; Mijolla, pp. 64-65.

Little Servants of Nazareth: Coste, "Piccole Ancelle di Nazareth," *Dizionario degli istituti di perfezione*, vol. 6, pp. 1584-1585.

Incorporating existing associations into the Marist confraternity:

LMA, docs. 2, § 1; 422, § 1-8; 431, § 28.

The Catechists of Mary, in Paris:

Sérol, "Le Rév. P. Alphonse Cozon," pp. 14-16, in *Physionomies maristes d'un premier siècle.* See also: "En marge du Tiers Ordre de Marie - L'œuvre des «Catéchistes de Marie» à Paris," *Les Annales de la Société de Marie*, 1 (1922): 348-355, 398-404; "Mlle Françoise de la Rupelle," *Les Annales de Marie*, 6 (1932): 345-360.

Index of Names

Subject Index